What Do You Learn In School?

How to Choose or Develop a Curriculum for
Church-Based and Home-School Teaching Programs

What Do You Learn In School?

How to Choose or Develop a Curriculum for
Church-Based and Home-School Teaching Programs

Brian Watts

DESTINY IMAGE EUROPE
Via Maiella, 1
66020 San Giovanni Teatino (Ch) - Italy
ISBN: 88-89127-05-8

First printing: 2004

This book and all other Destiny Image Europe books are available at Christian bookstores and distributors worldwide.

To order products, or for any other correspondence:

DESTINY IMAGE EUROPE

Via Acquacorrente, 6
65123 - Pescara - Italy
Tel. +39 085 4716623 - Fax: +39 085 4716622
E-mail: info@eurodestinyimage.com

Or reach us on the Internet:

www.eurodestinyimage.com

Contents

Foreword

Christian education had its beginnings centuries ago, but it was only in the past few decades that it grew into a worldwide movement. It was near the beginning of this period of phenomenal growth about thirty years ago that Brian Watts first caught a vision for Christian schools as an expression of the biblical mandate to train our children and disciple the nations.

Brian's vision did not remain just a "good idea" or theological concept; rather, it was tested in the rough and tumble of actual school life, emerging as a model that is solidly biblical and eminently practical. He learned as he furthered his biblical studies, and kept learning even as he taught students, parents, and teachers over the years.

I have known Brian Watts as a loyal, trusted friend for over twenty-five years. He is a man who loves the Word of God, who loves truth (at whatever cost), and whose gifting as a Bible teacher is increasingly appreciated and recognized.

Even while dealing with the "detail" that all good teachers must handle, Brian sees the "big picture" when it comes to Christian education: how family and church and school fit into God's plan. It is a vision that is set within the larger framework of God's covenantal plan and purposes—the goal of which is not ultimately the well-being of man, but the glory of God.

The history of Christian education also demonstrates its role in evangelism. Much church planting was preceded by Christian missionaries educating illiterate children, in turn attracting their parents who were impacted by the visible demonstration of the kingdom of God, and in time a church was born.

Today, the powerful effect of evangelism through education is also recognized by Islamic groups, whose schools and colleges are spreading rapidly throughout Africa and other parts of the world. It is from these Islamic-indoctrinated young people that terrorist groups like Al-Qaeda successfully gain recruits for their cause.

Meanwhile, Christian schools continue to emerge wherever the church is growing. Among our own family of churches, this includes India, Uganda, Burundi, Rwanda, Kenya, Northern Ireland, England, and Canada. In all of these countries (and certainly many others), Christian educators, parents, and church leaders will find this book of great benefit.

I believe that the formation of quality, Christian schools is a key, long-term strategy in training children as true "sons of the Kingdom" who love the Lord Jesus Christ and who are fully committed to His will and ways. If that is what you want for your children—if that is your vision for the young people of your church—I commend this book to you. You will be envisioned, inspired and encouraged in your efforts to faithfully train the children whom God has entrusted into your care.

Barnabas Coombs, President

Salt & Light Ministries and Church Relief International

Introduction

What do children need to learn in school? The word "school" conjures up a clear picture in our minds, an image drawn from childhood experience: chalkboards covered in exquisite cursive writing in 1st Grade, and incomprehensible scientific equations in 12th Grade. But where was the Word in the words?

As Paul told us, we are in urgent need of a radical renewing of our mind. That means, among other things, that we need to start to change our thinking about education. A biblical curriculum is different from a secular curriculum. Since *"The fear of the LORD is the beginning of knowledge"* (Proverbs 1:7), we should expect to find in God's Word all the leading ideas to direct the development of every branch of learning. In this book, we look forward to the day when our educators start with the Bible rather than the scope-and-sequence laid down in the government-run school system.

Most of the subjects in a traditional curriculum will appear in a Christian curriculum. But they may appear in a different context and with different priorities, and perhaps with different names to represent those distinctions. How about a lesson plan made up of subjects like Communication, Dominion Studies, Heritage Studies, Worship, Health, Government? These are subjects explored in the early books of the Bible, which was, after all, the first text-book of Jewish children in biblical times.

As we start to view curriculum through a Christian lens, we address some of the unsettling questions that emerge:

* If Jesus is "The Word," what do the Language Arts look like?

* Is it significant that History (His story) has been reclassified as Social Studies (our story)?

* If the Bible introduces Art in the context of worship, does that mean that art as self-expression is all about worshipping self?

* Could we count the number of apples in a basket if God were not a Trinity?

* Does the Bible teach us about building cities as well as churches? About money as well as faith?

This book is the first of a series of three books on Christian Education. The books are written for parents and teachers thinking about Christian schools and home-schooling programs as they start to question the life and teaching of the secular school system. In subsequent volumes we will look at:

* The Way to School: What school looks like in church-based and home-school teaching programs.

* Pupils who can See: What students look like in church-based and home-school teaching programs.

But in these chapters, our subject is what to teach. In *What Do You Learn in School?* we take a look at curriculum and examine how subject matter that is taught from a thoroughly biblical worldview will differ from the material presented in secular schools. What we learn should equip us for a life of victorious service for our King in whatever sphere he calls us to work.

Part 1

The Source of our Curriculum:

Christian Education Starts with the Bible as its
Foundational Textbook

Chapter 1

Changing How We Think

It's not *what* you know but *who* you know. This, we are told, is the key to getting ahead. In Christian education, *what* our children are expected to know is, of course, important. Educationalists call this the curriculum, the subject matter that needs to be mastered at each stage in a child's life. But the Bible says that *"The fear of the LORD is the beginning of knowledge"* (Proverbs 1:7); in other words, knowing God is the point of departure which establishes the direction for everything we know. *Who* we know affects *what* we know.

Does this mean that those who do not know God cannot know anything? In many ways this a hypothetical question, as Paul assures us that every human being knows God, for *"...what may be known of God is manifest in them, for God has shown it to them. For since the creation of the world His invisible attributes are clearly seen"* (Romans 1:19,20).

People, made in the image of God and daily confronted with the heavens that declare the glory of God, cannot escape the knowledge of God. He's everywhere! The problem, as Paul goes on to say, is that *"...although they knew God, they did not glorify Him as God"* (v. 21).

They chose to suppress the truth. It's not that people who exclude God from their thinking cannot know anything. But *what* they know is affected by their rejection of God.

Truth Decay

As everybody deliberately chooses to suppress the truth, Paul tells us, they become "...*futile in their thoughts*" (Romans 1:21). It is not that they cannot know anything, but everything that they know is somehow distorted. It's not so much *what* they know as what they *think* about what they know. Who you know determines what you think about what you know. An atheist and a Christian can both look at an apple and share much in common as to their knowledge of that piece of fruit—its chemical composition, the process of its propagation, its nutritional value, and so on. But for the atheist, the apple represents a chance product of an evolutionary process. For the Christian, the apple is part of the personal provision of a personal God who gives us all things freely to enjoy. Who you know radically affects how you think about what you know.

When the bell rings and we move from science class to social studies class, things get worse. It's people, not apples, who are now under the microscope. Are those people the chance product of slime plus time, or are they intricately formed handiworks of God, who knits each person together in a mother's womb? Viewed through each of these two lenses, history looks quite different, even if the characters and the events, the battles and the movements, are the same.

Countless Christian parents send their children to be taught in schools where the knowledge of God is excluded from the educational process. They assume that as long as their children are taught about apples (mathematics—how to count them; writing—how to spell them; science—how to analyze them; social studies—how to share them; and recess—how to eat them) that all will be well. And they assume that non-Christians are competent to instruct in such matters. But such parents fail to appreciate that education is about thinking as much as about knowing. And their children are not only being taught bare facts about apples; they are also being taught how to think about those apples. It is in this regard that *who* you know so vitally affects *what* you know. As a result, thousands of Christian children are daily "...*[sitting] in the seat of scoffers*" (Psalm 1:1), learning how to think—meditating—in the counsel of the ungodly.

It is against this backdrop that the Christian education movement is emerging. Whether in Christian schools or in home-schooling contexts, parents want to take a fresh look at what their children are learning. It's time to revisit the curriculum. It's time for a fresh look at what to learn, and especially what to think about what we learn.

Recently, a pilot was practicing high-speed maneuvers in a jet fighter. She turned the controls for what she thought was a steep ascent—and flew straight into the ground. She was unaware that she had been flying upside down. As Dallas Willard tells the story[1], he points out that it is a parable of human existence in our day: we live at high speed, and at times have no idea that we are flying upside down.

Nowhere is this more true than in our thinking. We live, we are told, in a post-modern era. While this is a culture in which our reliance on rationalism is now questioned, most of us still lean heavily on what the Bible calls "...*[our] own understanding*" (Proverbs 3:5). Perhaps, in these days, that understanding includes a measure of subjective intuition as well as cold logic, but it is our own understanding nonetheless, even if it is now usually couched in terms of "I feel" rather than "I think."

The jet pilot in the story made the classic mistake of "flying by the seat of her pants." Her instruments would have shown that she was flying upside down, but she had become disoriented through her high-speed maneuvers, and her senses told her that she was the right way up. Her fatal error was to trust her senses. She should have trusted the objective truth and the reliability of her instrument panel, regardless of what she "felt." This offers a salutary warning to all Christians who have the same tendency to fly by the seat of their pants, even if their feelings are formulated in the language of "The Lord told me to." To "follow your heart" can be a dangerous choice. In the sinfulness of our being, having spent a life doing maneuvers in a fallen world, we have become so disoriented that our heart cannot be trusted. The Bible says that our heart is deceitful (Jeremiah 17:9); it has an built-in bias toward misleading us.

When the Bible speaks of "the heart," it means something rather different than the way that we currently use the word. When we speak of the heart today, we are usually referring to our emotions. But when the Bible wants to speak of our emotions, it uses a different organ to describe their source: the bowels, though this is disguised in the more sensitive vocabulary used in our English translations. It may not look good on a Hallmark card, but a Hebrew Valentine card would have been more likely to say "I love you with all my bowels!" than "I love you with all my heart!"

In biblical times, the heart was seen as the source of all of life (Proverbs 4:23). It includes our mind and will as well as our emotions and intuitions. So when we are told to not lean on our own understanding (Proverbs 3:5), the instruction urges us not to follow our own heart (of which the understanding is a part); instead, our heart is to be trusting in the Lord. In terms of our flying analogy, rather than trusting our senses and our own judgement, we are to trust the objectivity of the instruments, the Lord himself, and his truth as revealed in the instrument panel of his Word.

This has significant implications for education. School is supposed to produce smart kids. Their teachers, as educated people themselves, are assumed to be smart. But the same series of Proverbs that has warned us not to rely on our own understanding goes on to say *Do not be wise in your own eyes*" (Proverbs 3:7). In other words, "Don't think you're smart!" We are to distrust our thinking, for it is part of the "heart" that has become disoriented by a life of maneuvers as a sinful being in a fallen world.

Distrusting our Thinking about Life

Our dilemma is that our thinking seems so normal to us. This is what makes the realm of education so critical. It is in our schooling that we are taught to think, and once we start to think in a certain way, we assume that that is the way to think. Everything we think about is understood in the framework of a way of thinking that we don't think about! But what if our thinking is wrong? The fact that Jeremiah tells us that our heart is deceitful, and that Paul tells us we are in urgent need of a radical renewing of our minds, suggests that we really are thinking "upside-down." This is especially true when the education system that has molded our thinking has been largely directed by those who have left God out of their thinking.

Most Christians are not deliberately trying to walk away from God, and they assume that the way they see reality is the way that reality really is. But Paul tells us, in effect, that the natural state of man apart from Christ is that of flying upside down while thinking we are flying the right way up. Paul describes this in terms of the "futility" of our minds, with our "understanding darkened" when we are alienated from the life of God; he describes us, apart from Christ, as being ignorant "...*because of the blindness of [our] heart*" (Ephesians 4:17,18). Since this is our natural state, he goes on to say that we must be "...*renewed in the spirit of [our] mind*" (Ephesians 4:23). The Christian life is the process of having our thinking straightened out so that we really know which way is up. That process can only effectively begin when we admit that, without the renewing work of the Holy Spirit, our disoriented hearts have led to an upside-down way of thinking.

This has implications for our approach to all of life, but our present concern is to see the implications for the realm of education. In our academics, as in all of life, we have become disoriented in our thinking. Since the Garden of Eden, mankind has both misunderstood creation and had a distorted view of the Creator. Those of us who grew up under teachers who did not acknowledge the truth about God and his Word need to be especially careful. Our thinking has been framed by the wisdom of the world (which Paul describes as the futile thinking of blinded hearts), so we need to check our natural tendency to "...*lean on our own understanding*" (Proverbs 3:5) and to trust what we think we know. And we should yearn for the prospect of our children learning about all of life with God at the center.

If we are to acknowledge Him in *all* our ways (Proverbs 3:6), we must look to Him as the One who has the wisdom to determine the best way to do math, the best way to understand language, the best way to approach teaching. And we dare not think that, because we are educated, we are smart ("*Do not be wise in your own eyes,*"—Proverbs 3:7a). Our smartness is tainted both by our own inward fallenness and the distorted training of "futile thinking." Instead, as the proverb goes on to say, we are to "...*fear the LORD*" (Proverbs 3:7b). It is the fear of the Lord that is the beginning of knowledge (Proverbs 1:7)—our academics start with God.

Since we as parents and teachers, and our children as students, are fallen creatures, the goal of Christian education is restoration. The great Christian poet John Milton wrote that the goal of learning "is to repair the ruins of our first parents." We need to have our thinking straightened out to the point where we can resume the task that God originally gave to mankind in the Garden of Eden. There, man was instructed to take dominion, to govern the earth to the glory of God (Genesis 1:26). The goal of Christian education is to equip children to be able to take their place in the spiritual warfare being waged for control of the planet. Mankind does exercise government over the earth in any case. But Christ came to restore humanity to its original dignity and purpose and to reverse the effects of the Fall so that those who are in Christ may be prepared to rule in a way that is pleasing to him.

Sadly, many who are turning toward some form of Christian education are more interested in pulling their children out of the battle so they don't get hurt in a hostile school. This may create a Christian ghetto, but not a true Christian education. Genuinely Christian education teaches children how to think, so as to be able to rule as they were created to do.

Distrusting our Thinking about Academics

We need to see the curriculum as the tool to rule. The foundation of all that is taught must be the Word of God. That does not imply that the Bible contains all the facts that must be taught. The fear of the Lord is the "beginning" of knowledge (Proverbs1:7): the word "beginning" implies that all the first principles, the leading ideas that will direct the development of every branch of learning, are found in Scripture. All our knowledge and all that we build with that knowledge has to be worked out in the context of the principles of God's Word as applied to each area. We start there rather than with our own understanding, or with the understanding that we have picked up from an education that is built on the "ignorance" that results from "alienation from the life of God."

When we look at the biblical origins of education, we find them rooted in the fact that God gave his people a curriculum in the Old Testament. The Bible, of course, is far more than that—but it includes this dimension, for there we find all that we need to know as a foundation on which to build our entire lives. We should not think of the Bible as only addressing so-called "spiritual issues;" God is in the business of teaching us about all of life, not merely things like how to run prayer meetings and take an offering.

According to Isaiah, God teaches us how to farm as well as how to pray (see Isaiah 28:23-29). As Isaiah describes a typical farmer's activities, he is clear that this was not learned in Agricultural School. How does the farmer know what to do?

[The Lord] instructs him in right judgment, His God teaches him (v.26).

We don't usually think of God as an agriculture instructor, but in the agricultural economy of biblical times the Jews needed to know that it was God who was their teacher in this most important area of life. The same is true in all aspects of learning that are important in any culture. God is our social studies teacher and our science teacher as much as he is our agriculture teacher. As Isaiah contemplates this fact, he concludes his meditation of how bread is made with a response of worship:

This also comes from the LORD of hosts, who is wonderful in counsel and excellent in guidance (v.29).

If God is the teacher who taught his people how to farm and how to make bread in an agricultural economy, in our day He is equally the One who teaches people how to be a plumber and how to make computers. We should not misunderstand this to mean that God teaches agriculture by means of some special revelation to farmers. Rather, by the image of God in man, man's ability to work is an aspect of his being and is a direct creative gift of God. We cannot separate any of our learning from God. As our teacher, he is the source of all our understanding. The passage in Isaiah makes it clear that he does not merely teach by imparting information in the general order of creation, but he also actively guides, adjusts, and corrects us as we go about our daily tasks. Work works best when we are in relationship with him. So, students need to learn that he is the source of all knowledge and that the application of that knowledge is not an academic exercise but an aspect of our daily relationship with the Lord. Most modern education is tantamount to flying upside-down because it does not start with the revelation that God is our teacher. All attempts at learning which exclude him will eventually lead to us "crashing the plane."

The Jews, without a Department of Education curriculum to guide them, started with their Bible. From earliest times, all the learning of Jewish children was explicitly based on the Law. It remained their curriculum well into the New Testament era when schooling was seen as part of the function of each local synagogue. Most people today would regard it as foolish to consider the books of Moses to be a foundational text book, but if we consider it as the "beginning" of knowledge (which is how it introduces itself in the very first verse), we find that we have here all the first principles upon which a curriculum is to be built—complete with a frame of reference as to why these areas are important to study. That is to say, it is the beginning of wisdom as well as of knowledge (see Proverbs 1:7; 9:10).

Christians in the New Testament era are not "under the Law" so far as our salvation is concerned. But the Old Testament speaks of much more than salvation. We usually think of salvation in the sense of personal forgiveness of sins and the restoration of an individual into a right relationship with God. But the Old Testament speaks also of the creation of a nation and a culture, and in the New Testament, the church continues this vision as the new Israel called out to do what the old Israel failed to do. While the New Testament brings vital new revelation concerning the meaning of salvation as it was only foreshadowed in the Old Testament rituals, it assumes that the principles of life already established for God's people remain valid. It was always God's intention to create in the Hebrew culture the ideal context into which his Son could be born and in which to flesh out his ideal for humanity. Insofar as that Hebrew culture accurately reflects the truths of God's law, it becomes a model for us, for it is the culture in which God in the flesh is seen. We disregard the Jewish view of education, the education by which the Lord Jesus in his humanity was trained, at our peril.

So, with this as our starting point, we turn to look at what a Christian curriculum might look like. What would our children learn if we started with the Bible rather than with the curriculum mandated by the secular educational authorities? Would they be as well equipped to face the modern world as their Jewish counterparts were to face their ancient world? If the Word of God is the starting point for all their thinking, they will be at least as well-positioned for a life of victory. And if their learning is pursued "in Christ," they will be "more than conquerors!"

ENDNOTES

1. Dallas Willard: The Divine Conspiracy (HarperSanFransisco; 1998) p.1

Chapter 2

A Bible-Based Curriculum

If we were not bound by a government-mandated curriculum, what would we teach? Most home-schooling parents and most Christian teachers do not start with this question. We usually begin with the curriculum already established in the public schools and then try to find a way to approach the same material in a Christian way. We are bound by the scope and sequence of the secular curriculum because we want our students to attain the recognition that graduation from the secular system affords.

But what if we could start again? If we could ignore the way things are and try to start from biblical principles, what would we teach? This requires a huge leap of imagination to try to think about what education might look like if our thinking were not dominated by school as we have known it. All kinds of things are up for debate: 6-hour days, 50-minute periods, summer holidays, age-segregated classes, final exams, grades. But for now we are focusing on the curriculum. What would our brand-new curriculum look like?

Most of the present subjects would appear, but they might appear in a different context and with different priorities, perhaps with different names to reflect those distinctions. What follows is a suggested outline that may provide a starting point for rethinking curriculum. It's the beginning of a dream for an entirely different kind of education.

1. Reading

Perhaps reading should be our starting point, for in the beginning is the Word. God is a God who speaks. In his wisdom he created the art of writing to ensure that what he has said may be clearly understood and remembered. The children of Israel often stood and listened to the law of God being read, and many times we are told that they were able to understand it. We stress the priority of reading because God has chosen to communicate in written form. Since that is the case, he clearly expects us to learn to read. Without this skill we will never be able to discern his principles upon which every other discipline is to be built.

Historically in Hebrew culture, Jewish children learned to read using the Scriptures, primarily the books of Moses, as their textbook. They began with the book of Leviticus: no pictures of Dick and Jane for them! They not only learned to read; they also learned that reading was important because it provided them access to the Word of God.

It is significant that God chose to communicate in words, as an outflow of his own nature which includes, in its Trinitarian expression, his being as the Word. The Old Testament is very clear that the Lord wanted his people to be distinct from the other nations in how they came to understand truth. The other nations all degenerated into visual cultures that were dependent on images, but Israel's understanding of their God, the true God, was dependent on words. He would not allow man to see him, but revealed himself verbally as the great I Am. Israel was forbidden to understand God visually, by depictions of his being in graven images. His revelation to them began with the significant phrase, "*Hear, O Israel.*" Theirs was a culture based on hearing the word, not seeing the image.

It is said that a picture is worth a thousand words, but the two simple words (in the English language) "I am" say much more than a thousand pictures could ever say about the nature of God. Profound theological truths about characteristics like immutability, self-sufficiency, and eternality are communicated with a precision and clarity that no visual representation could ever match.

This has come full-circle in our day. We too are faced with a culture, like those of the nations surrounding Israel, which is essentially visual rather than verbal. Jacques Ellul has developed a powerful critique of the theological significance of this trend in his important book, *The Humiliation of the Word*[1]. It is no coincidence that as our culture turns it back on God, literacy levels begin to drop. The spirit of the age is driving us away from the written word and toward the image. It may not be too alarmist to suggest that there is a demonic strategy behind this trend (after all, demonic strongholds primarily have to do with our minds, with ways of thinking, as Paul makes clear). A generation that cannot engage in serious reading will be unable to respond to a God who has chosen to reveal himself in a book. Yes, God has also revealed himself in a Person, Jesus Christ, but even there, it is a person who is known to us in a book, and a book which tells us what he said and did, but not what he looked like.

Reading in a Visual Culture

Reading is essential for being able to think the way God wants us to think, for God's thoughts are formulated and expressed in words. He could have inspired man to invent the technology of the video before developing the art of writing so that the record of his revelation were preserved in visual form. But visual communication develops different thought patterns: a series of immediate reactions to instantaneous images rather than a development of thought following a sequence of words. A generation that reacts to a series of visual images rather than following a train of thought has a hard time reading. It has a hard time thinking too.

It is not enough to say that we should adjust our teaching methods to suit a visual culture. This we have done with the use of videos, the bombardment of the senses with visual images in the classroom, and the radical change of textbooks from books that had a few illustrations to books that have a few captions to explain the pictures! The Reformers understood that the world needed to be able to read God's Word if they were to know the truth that would set them free from the tyranny of their day. With that in mind they set about translating the Scriptures and making them available to every person in their own language. But before that wonderful enterprise could be successful, they also had to embark on a massive program of teaching an illiterate culture how to read—otherwise their Bible translations would have had no success. We are in the same position. Our goal is to transform the culture to the point where people can again read and thus gain access to God's revelation in Scripture. While it is possible to use visual tools, this must never be an excuse for pampering a generation that does not want to read, thus leaving them in a place of being unable to relate to God in the way that He has chosen to relate to us.

Modern philosophical developments in the realm of language arts further detract from people's ability to respond to a God who speaks. These developments should be seen for what they are: a flight of rebellion away from God and reality as He has created it. Schools of thought like "Deconstructionism" are leading men to believe that language has nothing to do with discovering the original intent of the author; the focus has shifted to the side of the reader who can draw his own conclusions from the text. Ironically, the authors who write books about such ideas do expect you to be able to grasp *their* original intent when they are telling you that a reader cannot discern the original intent of an author! Christian education aims to produce children who are able to discern as accurately as possible what God has really said in His Word. A strong emphasis on phonics, spelling, and grammar serves such a commitment to precision and accuracy.

Young people who can neither read accurately nor continue to read thoughtfully through a whole argument, will be unable to grasp God's revelation. They will be satisfied instead in merely coming to their own conclusions, based on their own sensual impressions, as to what they think God might have said if He had been like them.

In our day, God has been re-created in our own image; a mental image constructed in our imaginations rather than in wood or stone, but an image nonetheless. The author Tolstoy once wrote:

"There are two Gods. There is the God that people generally believe in—A God *who has to serve them*[…] This God does not exist. But the God whom people forget—*the God whom we all have to serve*—exists."[2]

Setting reading as a foundation stone in the curriculum is essential to address this crisis. Only people who read and who think in such a way that their ideas of truth are formed by the revelatory Word will be able to know the God who really exists. Others will continue to recreate their own gods.

2. Writing

God made us to be like Him. One of the ways in which we are to be His image is to reflect His nature as God the writer. The Bible describes Him writing with His own finger on tablets of stone. The sanctifying work of the Holy Spirit is also an expression of God's penmanship as He "writes" His law on our hearts. Would it not have been wonderful to see God's handwriting on the tablets of stone that he gave to Moses? No spelling mistakes, no poor grammar, no sloppy handwriting. Why? Because any of those would have opened up the possibility that what He wrote was not accurately or easily understood.

Inaccuracy in writing leads to a loss of clarity in communication. One student's essay about William Tell makes the point. The student wrote of our hero that "he shot an arrow through an apple while standing on his son's head." A few carelessly misplaced words totally change the sense of what is being communicated. Using the wrong word has equally disastrous effects, as in the case of the student who wrote that the Constitution of the United States established "the right to bare arms." The modern dependence on "spell check" only aggravates the problem as we settle for offerings like this:

Eye strike a key and type a word

And weight for it to say.

Weather eye am wrong oar write

It shows me strait a weigh.

And these errors are justified by the defense that "My chequer tolled me sew!"

For the sake of clarity, God's Word was communicated in written form, and on numerous occasions, men and women were instructed to write down what they had heard or seen. The accuracy with which they were able to write was vital. Writing is important to God: he journals in "books of remembrance" when He is excited about something that He observes going on among His people (Malachi 3:16), and all the details of our lives will be laid bare for an entirely accurate judgment at the end of time when the records in His books are opened. There will be no inaccuracies in His books, for our eternal destiny is at stake in what He has recorded. He expects us to develop the same skills to enhance the clarity with which we can record, remember, and communicate. In His books, the focus is on truth and accuracy, precision and clarity. He is the starting point for the study of grammar and the reason for its importance.

We see this attention to precision in the care with which the scribes preserved the revelation of God's Word in their hand-written copies. The discovery of the Dead Sea Scrolls has confirmed how accurate the copying of manuscripts has been over the course of many centuries, so that we can be confident that the text in our modern printed versions is a reliable reproduction of the original documents. Josh McDowell details the process by which the Talmudists in and after the time of Christ ensured such accuracy[3]. Their orderly commitment to detail presents a challenging contrast to modern carelessness, but if we are as committed as they were to accuracy in communicating truth, their techniques would offer a fine example.

Telling Stories

But God is also a great storyteller. This is the source of all literature. He rarely communicates in a systematic list of principles. His principles are incarnated in the stories of people's lives (just as His Word is fleshed out in the person of His Son). Great storytellers are great communicators, but this is also becoming a lost art. The power of the written word rests in its interaction with our own imagination as we hear an author's words in our mind. By contrast, in a visual culture there is no comparable stimulus to develop the imagination: a visual image is handed to us on a plate, the photographic plate of our memories, as the movie producer instantly fixes the image in our minds. This requires no effort on our part, whereas our response to the word in story form plays a significant role in learning how to think. Words are tools in the hands of storytellers, and great craftsmanship makes it possible to powerfully communicate great truths in this way.

Literature is not about self-expression. God is the only being who can indulge in self-expression without being egotistical, —as John Piper makes clear in his book *The Pleasures of God: Meditations on God's delight in being God*[4]. Piper writes,

From all eternity God has beheld the panorama of his own perfections in the face of His Son. All that He is He sees reflected fully and perfectly in the countenance of His Son. And in this He rejoices with infinite joy. At first this sounds like vanity. It would be vanity if we humans found our deepest joy by looking in the mirror [...] But the same is not true for God. How shall God not insult what is infinitely beautiful and glorious? How shall God not commit idolatry? There is only one possible answer: God must love and delight in His own beauty and perfection above all things. For us to do this in front of the mirror is the essence of vanity; for God to do it in the form of His Son is the essence of righteousness.

As Piper points out, for God to focus on anything other than himself would be idolatry in that it would place the center of His contemplation on something less than His own perfection. Jesus is the Word, and as such is the ultimate self-expression of the God who is gloriously worthy to be revealed and expressed. His writing, in Scripture, is also fundamentally a means of self-expression, making himself known to a world that desperately needs to know the One who is worthy of our contemplation. But for us, if our art is a depiction of self for others to gaze upon, such a focus is idolatry—a drawing attention to that which is inferior, a distraction from the beauty of the One who is to be the center of our thoughts and worship.

We write, not for self-expression, but to bring glory to God, to communicate whatever is true, noble, just, pure, lovely, of good report, virtuous, and praise-worthy. We write in ways that are beautiful as an aid to help others to think about such things, to meditate on them, to fill their minds and imaginations with them, as we are exhorted to do in Philippians 4:8. Literature is an aid to meditation, a help to thinking; a means of musing. It helps us to fix our thoughts on the things that we ought to be thinking about. The modern pre-occupation is with *amusement*. This revealing word sums up the modern predicament: since the root of the word has to do with musing (thinking), this form of the word describes a negation of that pursuit. Amusement is literally not thinking. God shows us the better way in his definitive literary masterpiece. To a large degree, it is a book of stories; but it is a book to make us think.

It is also a book of poetry. We cannot understand the Bible if we do not appreciate poetry, for a quick skim through the layout of the pages of the Old Testament in particular will demonstrate how much God communicates in poetry. Adam gave us the first poem in history when he saw his wife for the first time (Genesis 2:23). When God cursed the serpent, he used the powerful medium of poetry to ensure that his words sank in (Genesis 3:14). The Holy Spirit is still interested in poetry. The first charismatic praise song was not a four line ditty; it was a beautiful poem (Luke 1:46-55). There is power in communication that is possible only in this form, and again a culture that is moving away from the written word is losing touch with the wonders of a God who speaks poetically and who also wants to use us as His mouthpieces.

3. Dominion Studies

The third discipline in our curriculum could be called Dominion Studies. It would include subjects such as mathematics and science. This was a priority in the curriculum that God created for Adam to follow in the school of life.

Mathematics

We are introduced to mathematics at the outset of the Bible. Perhaps we could argue that it came before literacy in the sense that our foundational phrase,"*In the beginning was the Word*," starts with a mathematical concept (beginning) rather than a language concept (Word)! Beginning implies order and sequence, and of course the account of creation develops this with our introduction to the world of numbers with the successive days of creation.

Mathematics would not be possible apart from God. His glory is inherent in every aspect of his creation, and it is that glory that enables us to engage in mathematical pursuits. His very nature as Trinity provides the foundation. In the Trinity we are introduced to what the philosophers have called "the One and the Many." God is One God: there is an essential oneness that means that when we think of Father, Son, and Holy Spirit, we must think of each of them as God. Yet there is also plurality within the Godhead: Father, Son, and Holy Spirit are each distinct persons to be known in their uniqueness, as well as in their unity within the single category of "God." Without the display of perfect balance between these two aspects (the one and the many) in God, mathematics would be incomprehensible in a world created in any other way.

Observe how this important revelation of the Trinity is fundamental to even the simplest mathematical task. Imagine a pile of apples on a desk: the challenge before our young student is to count the apples. Each of the apples is unique in size and shape and color, reflecting the distinctiveness of the three persons of the Trinity. Yet there is a oneness about them; for all their differences, they all fall into the category of "appleness." You can count apples because all apples, however different, are apples. If they weren't all apples you could not do the simple mathematical procedure of adding them. Without the foundational principle of oneness, how would you know what, of all the things on the desk (five apples, an eraser, a pen, three pieces of paper, a dead fly, and a billion dust particles) could be added together? Yet if they were not distinct, they could not be added either. The number five has no meaning in a mystical eastern world where all is absorbed in the great amorphous oneness.

And we wonder why math scores are dropping! Teachers without the philosophical foundation of the truth of the Trinity have no basis for doing mathematics. We are introduced to this right at the beginning of the Bible. Just as there is one God and yet distinct persons, so there could be six distinct days of creation, yet each of them could be handled as a single category since each could be considered as a "day." This shows that there can be a mathematical relationship (first, second, third...) between different yet related items.

Consider some of the mathematical-theological implications introduced in the first chapters of the Bible. The Bible begins with the measurement of time. Creation starts with a void, setting "zero" at the beginning of the number line. Then the evening and morning were the first day. God uses an ordinal number, a number that denotes order in a given series, to express His measurement of time. It denotes the character of the day (a period of time) and begins a sequence that the Bible tells us will one "day" come to an end, completing the measurement of time. God stands above His creation as the ultimate Judge: He is the One who defines and measures time. All is related to His divine time-line and is measured according to a divine standard.

In Genesis 1, God created light and *divided* the light from the darkness, the first division. He created the sun and moon, the *greater* and *lesser* lights, the first inequalities. He created living creatures with the command to be fruitful and *multiply*, the first multiplication. He himself defines the hugeness of infinity, yet He is so personal that He will not miss the fall of a sparrow, valued in monetary terms at a fraction of the value of a man. He takes delight in counting the number of hairs on our heads!

Just as language exists as a revelation of the nature of God, so does mathematics. We read that God is a God of order and thus expects that everything we do be done "...*decently and in order*" (1Corinthians 14:40, emphasis added). God's Word is His primary means of self-disclosure, but His invisible nature is also seen in all that He has created (Romans 1:20). Just as we speak of computer programming "languages," so we may think of mathematics as the language with which He constructed His creation. Mathematics is now the language that man uses to understand that creation. In turn, it is to be a language by which we understand our Creator.

Science and Vocational Training

There is much more that could be said about the relationship between math and theology, but for now we take it into another realm. Mathematics becomes a foundation for what we now call science: the process of understanding the Creator as seen in His creation. This enquiry began in the Garden of Eden.

Man was instructed at the outset to "name" the creatures in God's creation (Genesis 2:20). This was far more than "labeling" them elephant or monkey or whatever arbitrary label Adam could come up with. It was a commission to study in order to understand the essential nature of God's creatures. But naming speaks of even more than understanding the inner nature; it is also a function of dominion. When a man calls his dog *Fido*, an authority structure is established—it is the man who is naming the dog, not the dog who is naming the man! So the naming process upon which Adam embarked was an expression of his mandate to subdue the creation. As his understanding grew, his ability to classify enhanced his ability to harness the raw material that God had placed at man's disposal in the mandate of dominion.

Initially, subjects like math and science were pursued in the context of providing shelter (note the stress on dimensions in the Ark) and agriculture. Industrial arts were also an early part of man's fulfillment of the Dominion Mandate (Genesis 4:22). Carpentry, mechanics, and other such disciplines fit into the curriculum here: they are part of equipping young people to take their place in the work-force, which is an expression of the task of dominion. Adam's calling was in a garden, but this becomes a symbol of every area of productive work. Thus Career Guidance and Vocational Training courses become part of the preparation of young people to take dominion in the various spheres to which they are called.

The task given to Adam and his descendants was ultimately to construct a city: a civilization built to the glory of God out of all the raw materials that God had provided. Interestingly, in Genesis 2:8-15 we have a list of some of the raw materials made available to man for this enterprise. At the "end of the story," those resources are seen again, but now in a fully-built city rather than buried in the ground. In Revelation 21 and 22, we read of the finished product. It is a city of heavenly origin, but it is found on earth.

The fall of man marred the process of scientific discovery. Man stopped acting as steward of God's creation, ruling to God's glory. Instead, he began to exploit it to his own ends; he began to build the city of man rather than the city of God. In a Christian curriculum, mathematics and science are to be directed toward reclaiming a biblical focus for dominion, a focus for which the whole creation groans in anticipation (Romans 8:19-22). The principles of dominion are all available, and we are guaranteed an orderly world by a God of order who has established laws and uniformity so that there can be a measure of certainty in the regularity of nature, as promised in his declaration:

> *While the earth remains, seedtime and harvest, cold and heat, winter and summer, and day and night shall not cease* (Genesis 8:22).

In other words, scientific exploration is possible because of who God is. The only question is what we will do with what God has given us.

4. Heritage Studies

In the fourth area of a curriculum that starts with the Bible, we find subjects such as history and geography. These have been terribly distorted in modern education, where they have been renamed in a newly invented category called social studies. The new category significantly suggests that they have to do with the study of man rather than the study of God. History (His story) has become social studies (our story). Interestingly, literature, as we shall see, might also feature in this part of the curriculum.

God was always concerned that His people remembered His works of old. Jewish children raised on the textbooks of Genesis to Deuteronomy would have picked up God's concern in this regard (e.g. Exodus12:24-27). In fact, much in these books focuses on the need for God's people to understand the *future* inheritance that he has for them in light of their *past* heritage.

He is a God who not only speaks in commandments and principles, but also in real-life geographical and historical contexts, establishing principles in narratives and stories. Unless we understand the context (geography and history), we will misunderstand the message of God's providential dealings. Interestingly, the Jews referred to the historical books in Scripture as the "former prophets;" they recognized that God was speaking in the events of their history. God speaks in His "Word;" God speaks in mathematical language; God speaks in history.

Past events came to life with present relevance in the literary skills with which men of God communicated God's Word in story form (narrative, not fiction). The principles were fleshed out in people's lives, recorded and described for subsequent generations to appreciate. Here we learn that history apart from literature will bore a generation with dates and facts, but Jewish history, while showing a relative disregard for dates, powerfully inspires young people with heroes and adventures. The novels of a writer like G.A. Henty, written for young boys a hundred years ago, are somewhat old-fashioned in their depiction of great historical events, but they are much closer to following a biblical pattern than many modern approaches. And they were truly successful in raising a generation that was historically literate in comparison with most moderns who have little knowledge of life before the invention of the television!

Similarly, geography comes alive when seen as a further revelation of God's nature. Note the way the Bible speaks of such things as wind, rain, rivers, and rocks as full of theological implications. It is the stage that he has set to act out the drama of history. Looking at God's creation in the world around us, we are reminded that wind and water, and all the powerful forces that have shaped the contours of the physical landscape are not the result of merely physical laws. This is not an impersonal world. God is at work in even the so-called "natural" events (e.g. Psalm 135: 6,7; 147:15-18). It is not futile to pray for rain or for sunshine. The totally predictable expectations of science must bend to accommodate the possibility of unexpected answers to prayer. The world is studied as a place where God continues to be at work, not merely as an old, long-finished masterpiece to be admired in its antiquity.

We need to know about the history of Israel, but we also need to understand God's providential dealings in our own heritage and the contrast that this presents with other cultures and civilizations. A generation that forgets its heritage, that loses its awareness of its past as the acts of God, is destined for trouble (Judges 2:10). Certainly this is true in the rootlessness of a "now" generation that only exists in the existentialist "now" and has little respect for its elders ("What can we learn from *them*? They didn't even have computers back then!") It is no coincidence that the history of western civilization is being erased from the memory of modern students. Course after course is being eliminated from university programs. They are being replaced with new social studies programs consistent with a modern agenda of social engineering: gender studies, courses accentuating other civilizations, and so on. Christian education must rediscover and redefine heritage studies.

5. Worship

Worship was an important item in the curriculum of young Jewish children. Approaching their curriculum as they did, through the text of God's Word, it would have been in this context that they would have been introduced to subjects such as music and art. In fact, it would have been strange to them to think about such subjects in any other context.

While man has used artistic skills to try to create his own reality, the Old Testament curriculum is clear that the arts fall into the realm of worship. Artistic skills are gifts of the Holy Spirit, not merely human genius. Musicians take their place in the worship services of the Tabernacle and artistic craftsmen, filled with the Holy Spirit, make the tabernacle and the worship of God's people a thing of beauty.

Art and Worship

This does not mean that art is only valid when it is filled with religious words. A picture with a text on it hanging on a bedroom wall may be poor art (as is much that is sold in what used to be Christian bookstores on shelves that used to contain books!) A song with Christian words may have weak lyrics and be recorded by a second-rate musician. It is certainly not "Christian content" that makes art good art. Countless paintings hanging on the walls of the world's great art galleries are great art even if they do not depict religious scenes, and marvellous symphonies have no religious words yet resound with artistic excellence. But still, I would suggest, even these non-religious works fit into the category of worship. How so?

Art has to do with drawing our attention to beauty and then directing that attention to the Creator. The beauty may be visible or audible; it may be tactile or gastronomic. But whatever its form, it is a matter of taking the beauty of God's creation and fashioning it skillfully in a way that brings pleasure to man and glory to God.

Art is not ultimately a matter of creativity. Genesis uses the word "create" very sparingly, and only to refer to the direct activity of God when He creates something out of nothing (matter, life, and the human spirit). Everything else is described in terms of God "made" or "formed"—i.e. as a craftsman He fashioned new things out of existing materials. The fact that man is made in the image of God does not make him a creator. We have no power to make anything out of nothing, for even that which is uniquely the product of our own imagination comes out of a mind that has been formed by the input of others and using materials that we bought at the store!

Modern man, in his desire to be as God, yearns to be considered as "creative," proudly assuming that he can create his own reality out of himself. But the biblical model of art is a more modest endeavor: man made in the image of God the craftsman. God the Creator is also God the craftsman: the One who takes previously created materials and, using great skill, makes incredible new variations, at the completion of which He can step back and say, "Wow! That's good!" In the creation story, that positive assessment brings glory to the God who does all things well. Similarly, at the end of our art, the expressions of appreciation about how good a piece is should similarly bring glory to the God who has made the raw materials and acknowledge the skills of the artist who rearranged the elements of creation in such a beautiful way.

Take the realm of music as an example. One can sit back at the end of a Beethoven symphony, even if it has no Christian lyrics and was written by a man whose life was fraught with all kinds of anti-Christian tensions, and say, as God did at the end of each of the days of creation, "That's good!" Such a statement need not be blasphemous—though it may be, if our "worship" is directed to the composer or the orchestra. Remember, Jesus said we cannot describe anyone or anything but God as truly "good" (Mark 10:18)! The symphony is good in the sense that a man has taken his God-given skills to explore the wonderful world of God-created sounds. He has produced a piece of music that we enjoy with a pure enjoyment that causes us to say "What a wonderful world! What a wonderful God!" All creation (sight, sound, touch, and taste) declares God's praise, and artists, whether landscape gardeners or gourmet chefs, symphony composers or still-life painters, textile designers or interior decorators, take God's creation and frame it in such a way that we can focus and enjoy it, culminating in the almost involuntary exclamation, "Wow!" It is that "Wow!" which is really an expression of worship; the only question is whom we are worshipping.

Popular Art

That is not to say that the only valid expression of art in the musical realm is the high-end culture of the great orchestras. The Bible also speaks of music in a variety of other non-religious expressions at a more popular level. For example, we find music as an expression of patriotism in the Bible. Again this is a matter of worship, but capable of being used in the worship of different gods—either a man-centered worship in nationalism (as was clearly seen in the Third Reich), or a God-focused worship when patriotism is an expression of gratitude for a God-given heritage. We are supposed to feel emotional when we sing our national anthem in a crowded sports arena and be inspired to fight for our country as we sing on our way to the battlefield in a just war.

Similarly, there are biblical examples of music as simple love songs. We do not need to make the words "I love you!" ambiguous, as modern religious artists sometimes try to do in composing a song that can be sung both to a human lover and to God. The problem with much modern music is not its preoccupation with love and romance, for mankind always has and always will sing love songs. The Bible has love songs (e.g. Song of Solomon) that are every bit as sensual as many modern songs. The difference is that modern culture takes such songs as an expression of worshipping the ideal of human freedom, men and women freed from the restraints of God-given standards. Biblical love songs express love in the context of the sanctity of marriage within which sensuality is an expression of worship to God, who has provided so richly for our pleasure within the boundaries of His loving will, and in His provision of a spouse, for He knows it is "not good for a man to be alone."

Most cultures view art as an expression of worship. The highly decorative arts of India arise out of a culture in which they form part of the worship of a multitude of gods. The characteristic designs of North American Indian art revolve around the creatures and the spirits that have been part of their religious traditions for centuries. It is only in relatively modern western art that we have tried to maintain a separation between art and spirituality. Naturalism replaced the depiction of biblical themes. But rather than reflecting a separation between art and worship, this merely reflects a change in the object of our worship. Where once art was a medium for expressing the worship of God, in western culture man and nature have become the new gods, and art has changed to reflect these new deities.

Some artists deliberately try to express this sense of the divinity of man in their desire to create their own reality. Sometimes, even with Christian musicians singing so-called worship lyrics, a performer uses his art to foster personal adulation. Sometimes the yearning for "self-expression" reflects a desire to draw attention to "self" as if a multitude of people really need to know what's going on inside of me. Sometimes the god is the god of Mother Nature rather than the individual self. But all such activities are essentially spiritual. They are all an expression of worship: the only questions are "To which god?" and "By which spirit?"

Spiritual Art

It is significant that the early Old Testament curriculum describes art as a distinctly spiritual task. Bezalel is one of the first people to be called

"Spirit-filled." For him this was in the realm of art, but it was just as clearly a manifestation of the Holy Spirit as that by which Moses was anointed to be the spiritual leader of the nation (see Exodus 35:30—36:8). A couple of points arise that need further development:

Firstly, the nature of art was distinctive in Hebrew culture. In Part Three, we will describe the contrast between Greek and Hebrew culture, with the implications for our philosophy of education. Nowhere is this more profound than in the realm of art. For example, Bezalel was not sculpting statues of nude figures, as became common in Greek culture. In fact, he was not even free to create his own designs; the focus was on his craftsmanship and his obedience to produce beautiful, decorative materials following designs precisely given by God. The content of his artwork and the characteristics of beauty, of decorative design, and of obedience (rather than self-expression) form the basis of an interesting study on the foundations of a biblical approach to art.

Secondly, Bezalel's art was an expression of the "spirit" within him. Gordon Fee has done a massive study on all the references to "spirit" in the writings of Paul[5]. One of his conclusions is that when we read the word "spirit," the reference is usually not to the "human spirit." In a Christian context, it almost always refers to the Holy Spirit. Our culture, with its distinctively modern stress on human spirituality, has become less familiar with the idea of "spirit" as an external personality rather than as a part of who we are. But Paul is equally clear that those who are not Christians are driven to a large measure by external spiritual forces (*"The spirit who now works in the sons of disobedience"*— Ephesians 2:2).

It would seem that the reference to Bezalel's artistic genius in terms of being "filled with the Spirit of God" as opposed to merely human creativity opens up interesting questions about the nature of art. Art is an expression of spirituality, and perhaps not so much the spirituality of the human spirit as other spirits at work in humans. The result is that other gods are worshipped.

It is again shocking to think what parents might be exposing their children to when they are sent to sit in "the seats of scoffers" in art classes in many secular schools. Which gods are being glorified? They may be internal gods of self or external gods of human imagination or demonic origin. Which spirits are being invoked as the genius behind such art? They may be human spirits, "the muse," or even demonic powers. Christian art expresses worship to God insofar as it is inspired by the Holy Spirit. In Christian education, the art curriculum must be developed in the context of obedience to God, the importance of the work of the Holy Spirit who only operates in the context of bringing glory to Christ, and of worship as a full-orbed activity that goes far beyond the singing of religious songs. It is time to reorient our upside-down thinking about art.

6. Health

This sub-section of a biblical curriculum covers subjects such as nutrition and hygiene (Home Economics) and Physical Education. Large portions of the Old Testament law, which formed the basis for a Hebrew model of education and which could serve us equally well, were devoted to this important area. Since these books were written, our detailed scientific knowledge of such matters has increased, as God intended it to as humanity pursued the dominion mandate. The ceremonial aspects of laws regarding foods have clearly been superseded by the New Covenant. But the regulations given in these books still contain valid principles which demonstrate God's concern with our physical bodies as well as with our spiritual health.

As we integrate modern scientific understanding and New Testament revelation into these principles, our care for our bodies is developed in the context of such ideas as the sanctity of life and of our bodies being a temple of the Holy Spirit. The value of bodily exercise is held in balance with the pursuit of godliness. The demonic distortions of God's purposes for food are spelled out (1 Timothy 4:1-5). But food plays a large part in the life of God's people. We know little about fasting and equally little about feasting in the way that the Bible places an equal emphasis on both.

The Bible has some interesting insights into practical issues like eating disorders. At the "under-eating" end of the spectrum, we find that a Hebrew view of beauty is wildly at variance with the modern picture of waif-like models. A Hallmark Valentine's Day card in biblical times would have included such choice lines to one's wife as *"My darling, your belly is like a heap of wheat!"* (Song of Solomon 7:2)

Solomon was less focused than we might be on her physical appearance; it is modern western thinking that focuses on visual image. To Solomon, it was this woman's fruitfulness that was important, whether in her ability to have children or to live a productive life. He was not necessarily describing her shape! Similarly, he wrote, "Your neck is like the tower of David, built for an armoury, on which hang a thousand bucklers, all shields of mighty men." It was enough to make a Hebrew girl go weak at the knees, for she understood from Solomon's love language that he valued her strength. There was much more to attractiveness than outward appearance as defined by the latest fashion magazine. In such a curriculum there is no pressure toward thinness as a virtue.

Similarly, at the "over-eating" end of the spectrum of eating disorders, our culture reflects that upside-down thinking in which we are driven by our senses to destruction. In our culture, when people need comfort or need cheering up, their first resort is often the fridge; Hebrews tells us, our first resort should be the throne of grace.

We read that,

It is good that the heart be established by grace, not with foods (Hebrews 13:9).

Today, food has become an alternative to grace, but as the verse in Hebrews goes on to point out, it ultimately proves unable to help. It is impossible to fully deal with eating disorders without providing ways to access God's grace. Again, a Christian curriculum can deal with all areas of our lives in this holistic way.

7. Government

Finally, our perusal of the first five books of the Old Testament will lead us to realize that God has a lot to say about civil government. The New Testament says relatively little about this, but it doesn't need to say more since God's Word already contained the fundamental principles. God's ancient people, the Jews, give us the first indication of how those principles might be fleshed out in a particular civilization. Our culture is not theirs, but the principles of God's Word are eternal, and it is our task to see how they are to be applied in our day.

In studying government we are introduced to subjects such as law, criminology, economics, and the military. God's Word is not purely personal. God is interested in saving souls, but the reduction of the gospel to the purely personal, individualistic level is one of the major areas where our thinking has been distorted by modern western philosophies. His goal is to build a city, not merely save souls. He is at work to restore creation, not merely to get saved souls to heaven.

There is no area of social and corporate life for which He has not laid the first principles of our knowledge in the Scriptures. They become our starting point to examine critically every human departure from these principles in the realm of public policy. And we must be critical, for apostate man has been trying to build a city apart from God ever since the days of Babel, right down to all the modern Babylonian counterparts which seem as impressive as the Tower of old, but which are equally vulnerable and short-lived.

In previous generations, those who wanted to train as lawyers first had to complete their studies in theology; they understood then that the Bible was the basis of our legal system. That is rapidly changing, but the replacement that is being constructed cannot last. Anything—including a nation's legal system—that is not built on the foundation of doing what God says must disintegrate. As Jesus said of such constructions,

> *The rain descended, the floods came, and the winds blew and beat on that house; and it fell. And great was its fall* (Matthew 7:26,27).

Our goal is to train a generation of young people who can build on God's Word and who will be part of the solution to the coming crises in our culture.

It is shocking to evangelicals to discover that the Bible has more references to money than it has to faith. So why would we look anywhere else for our economics foundations? And as the world wrestles with whether the USA has the right or the responsibility to invade Iraq (or any other threatening nation), few people ask, "What does the Bible say?" Yet the Old Testament has much to say about the nature of warfare and its legitimate and illegitimate expressions. David was a man after God's heart, but he was also a man of war (1 Samuel 16:18)—hardly the pastoral, harp-playing aesthete sitting on the hillside counting sheep! Yet it is not incongruous that a man of war should also be a man after God's heart, for God is described as "a man of war" (Exodus 15:3).

While the issue of pacifism is obviously a contentious and complicated issue, we can at least agree that David was a man after God's heart, for even in his position as a civil ruler he sought to subject his decision-making process to the will of God. He did not go to war on a whim; he is repeatedly described as enquiring of the Lord before engaging in a battle (e.g. 1 Samuel 30:8). When he wrote that God's Word was a lamp to his feet, he was not thinking in purely personal or devotional terms. God's Word directed his policy as a king as much as his personal life. That is why God instructed kings to be familiar with the first books of the Bible, our basic curriculum. They were expected to be ruled by it and to rule by it (Deuteronomy17:14-20).

Our goal in Christian education is to produce good citizens as well as good church members. Godly Christian schools and home-schooling parents need to produce politicians as well as pastors. But in both spheres, God's Word reveals God's will: the way God wants us to live in every area of our life. This is the kingdom of God—everything being done on earth the way God does things in heaven.

All that we do in Christian education flows out of a divinely inspired curriculum. It is based on our theology of creation, which gives us the reason for and the boundaries of all scientific inquiry within the Dominion Mandate. It is based on a theology of Theism that requires God's active involvement in His entire creation, upholding all things by His powerful word. It is based on a theology of providence that tells us that God is actively working all things together for good in a time/space world. It is based on a theology of the word that recognizes that communication is at the heart of God's being and integral to the nature of man made in the image of God. It is based on a theology of worship that puts God at the center of all things and demands that all things exist for His glory.

Any curriculum that is not undergirded by these theological presuppositions is bound to fail. We start with the fear of God, and if we are off course at the start of our studies, we will be lost before we finish. It is vital that Christian educators go back to first principles in rewriting curriculum. And it is vital that all Christian parents carefully examine the foundations of all that their children are being taught.

With these first principles in place, we can begin to build an approach to education with its goal being, as Harvard University once proclaimed, "to know God and Jesus Christ, which is eternal life, and therefore to lay Christ in the bottom as the only foundation of all sound knowledge and learning."

ENDNOTES

1. Jacques Ellul: The Humiliation of the Word (Grand Rapids:Eerdmans; 1985)

2. Quoted by Dallas Willard: Renovation of the Heart (Colorado Springs: NavPress; 2002)

3. Josh McDowell: Evidence that Demands a Verdict (Campus Crusade for Christ; 1972) p.56,57

4. John Piper: The Pleasures of God (Sisters OR: Multnomah; 1991) p.38,39

5. Gordon Fee: God's Empowering Presence (Peabody MA: Hendrickson; 1994)

Part 2

The End of our Curriculum:

Christian Education Recognizes no
Secular/Sacred Divide

Chapter 3

The Goal of Christian Education

Curriculum is a course of study. What's the end of the course? What is the primary purpose of Christian education? The overall goal of *everything* we do is to be the glory of God. "The chief end of man is to glorify God and enjoy Him for ever" (Westminster Shorter Catechism). As Paul puts it,

> *Whether you eat or drink, or whatever you do, do all to the glory of God* (1 Corinthians 10:31).

Since we are to do "everything" for God's glory, even eating and drinking, parents have a responsibility to ensure that their children's education is for God's glory. Genuine Christian education must be distinct from education in a secular school.

The Hebrew word for "glory" is *kabod*, which means, "to be heavy." Paul had this Hebrew concept in mind when he wrote of an "...*eternal weight of glory*" (2 Corinthians 4:17). It may seem strange to think of weight or heaviness in relation to God, but we can perhaps understand this in terms of the modern idiom in which we say that something "carries weight." We realize that, in our desire to glorify God, we cannot make

Him any heavier, for He already possesses an infinite weight of goodness, majesty, power, honor, and so on. But to "glorify God" is to ascribe to Him the full weight of all the qualities that He already possesses. So, as Jay Adams writes, "To do everything (math included) for God's glory is to do it in such a way that the full weight of God's relationship to it is acknowledged."[1]

To the humanist, God is a "lightweight." He is regarded as insignificant in the various disciplines of education. Everything is viewed apart from God; weight is given to man instead. But in Christian education we must give full weight to God's part in all that we study. His claims and his revelation truly carry weight in *what* we teach and *how* we teach. The purposes of Christian education revolve around enabling students to understand and relate to God in all that they do. Weight is given to God's revealed purpose for mankind, for human beings only truly glorify God when they give due weight to what He says their life is all about.

The Great Commission—in Two Parts

God's purpose for man was established in the Garden of Eden, where the Lord laid out for Adam what he expected of him and his descendants:

> *Be fruitful and multiply; fill the earth and subdue it; have dominion over the fish of the sea, over the birds of the air, and over every living thing that moves on the earth* (Genesis 1:28).

This commission has been variously described as the Dominion Mandate or the Creation Command.

Most Christians, if asked what our purpose is, would probably turn to Matthew 28:18-20, which has been labelled "The Great Commission." That would be accurate. But we must see that the two commissions (in Genesis 1 and in Matthew 28) need to be taken together.

The Great Commission of Matthew 28 is vital given the sad reality that Adam's fall embroiled humanity in sin long before the Dominion Mandate could be fulfilled. The crying need of a fallen world is for the spread of the gospel of Jesus Christ, though we should note in passing that Jesus described this gospel as the "gospel of the kingdom," not as the gospel of personal salvation. But the Great Commission does not replace the Dominion Mandate. It merely restates the theme that God longs for the world to be filled with people who love him. Both Adam and Jesus' disciples were to "be fruitful and multiply." Once people have been saved from the snare of sin by the power of the gospel, they are then restored to the place where they can again start to fulfill God's original purpose of subduing the earth in a way that brings glory to God.

If we see the Great Commission as the end of our discussion of human purpose, rather than the starting point, we are left with a very incomplete and largely ethereal (some would say spiritual) reason for our existence. We are to make disciples, teaching them "...*to observe all things that I have commanded you.*" Some have said that the "things that I have commanded you" are simply the instructions of the Great Commission itself. That is to say, the Great Commission tells us to make disciples, teaching them in turn to make disciples who can also make disciples. Certainly this would satisfy the "be fruitful and multiply" part of the original mandate. But can this be all that Jesus meant when He said that these disciples are to be taught to observe "all things that I have commanded you"? Surely "all things" includes everything He has asked of us from Genesis to Revelation, not merely all the things that He said in Matthew 28:18-20.

The Great Commission includes the mandate to make disciples who are able to observe the "subdue creation" as well as the "be fruitful and multiply" dimensions of what the Lord commanded at the very beginning. This is important for Christian education, for it is Jesus who has defined what it is we are to teach. Our curriculum is defined in Matthew 28. We are to teach students (disciples) to observe all the things that Jesus has commanded them.

If we reduce "all things" to a narrow band of so-called "spiritual" observances (how to be a fruitful witness, how to read the Bible, how to pray, etc.), then Christian teaching becomes largely confined to the four walls of our church buildings and has essentially been accomplished in Sunday Schools. Consequently, and sadly, teaching about the rest of life is then left to the secular "Monday through Friday schools." Even in the USA, blessed with so many fine Christian schools and home-schooling resources, 80-90% of students from church homes still go to public schools.[2] We let the world teach our children about the rest of life, and the world has been very effective at teaching a humanist version of the Dominion Mandate, even to our own church members. Do not be deceived: the world has its own visions of the purpose of man's life in the world. It too pursues dominion.

Made to Rule

Teaching people to observe what the Lord has commanded begins with His first command in Genesis. This was not merely a personal instruction to Adam. The words of Genesis 1:28 are addressed to "them" even though Adam was the only human being alive at the time: this was God's command for mankind as a whole, not merely for a particular man. There was a moral aspect to God's instructions, expressed negatively in the command concerning forbidden fruit. But in the Dominion Mandate the focus is on man's calling to work. Adam's personal task was to till the Garden, and this was representative and symbolic of every sphere of work to which we are all called.

Sin subsequently changed the dynamics of work and radically distorted what man does with his labors, but it did not negate the command initially given. For thousands of years, mankind has continued to take dominion over the created order, just as certainly as people have also been fruitful and multiplied! Every scientific advance, every cleared field, every house constructed, testifies to the fact that when God spoke to Adam it was with words that were not merely heard with his ears, but with words that were written into man's genetic make-up. Man was made to rule. Sin did not change the fact that man was to rule. It simply meant that he began to rule badly. He exercised the authority, but did so in violation of his responsibility to rule to the glory of God.

With sin effectively dealt with in Christ, Christians are restored to the place where we can fruitfully revisit that first instruction. The Great Commission takes us back to the Creation Command. As Adam was given a "garden," so each of us is entrusted with a sphere for rule to God's glory.

Since man was made to subdue the earth, this becomes the focus of our curriculum. In Adam's day, there were few resources and minimal manpower immediately available. The manpower shortage was addressed by the command to multiply. The resources, while largely hidden, were available; they had been provided by God, buried in the earth. They were simply waiting to be uncovered and utilized. Skills for the task were slowly developed over time, and the understanding necessary to fulfil the task also grew slowly. That process of a growing workforce, discovering new resources, developing new skills and ever increasing understanding will continue throughout human history until God's purposes are fulfilled.

And all education, in one way or another, should further this mandate of dominion as given at the time of creation.

Ruling the Earth to Glorify God

The major goals of education revolve around teaching people how to rule over creation. That means dealing with worldwide problems such as global warming, with national problems like an overheating economy, or with domestic problems such as an overheating radiator. In Christian education, we seek to train young people to rule as God has commanded us, in ways that truly glorify Him. There are many facets to this. We can perhaps summarize them under two headings.

Firstly, God knew that it would take many people to subdue the earth, hence the command to multiply. The earth could only be subdued by a co-operative venture in which all play their part harmoniously. Interpersonal relations—people skills—are vital. People are required to develop ways of relating to one another according to biblical principles in order to get the job done. Education must focus on all aspects of human relationships in a variety of group settings, such as family, society, politics, business, and church. In addition, it must teach students how to relate in issues like forgiveness, kindness, and servanthood.

Secondly, education must address the need for the study of animate and inanimate objects—the things which are to be subdued. Psalm 8:6 summarizes the human calling as *"You have put **all things** under his feet."* Adam's education began with an investigation into the animal kingdom: "naming the animals" (Genesis 2:19,20) and seeking to identify the nature of each as a vital first step in the process of subduing them. But the inanimate creation was also part of Adam's mandate. There was a wealth of resources that the Lord had deposited (e.g. Genesis 2:11,12) and there was a need to both care for the Garden and subdue the wilderness.

Fulfilling the Great Commission—for Good or Evil

Sin ruined what mankind did with this mandate. But it is no coincidence that when the Bible gives us a summary of Adam's son Cain (Genesis 4:16-24), it not only includes a description of the moral failure that unfolded, but also the progress in "subduing" that emerged. In essence, mankind took two steps back but one step forward. A city was built. New developments in residential housing, livestock management, and musical instruments are recorded (Genesis 4: 20,21). Significantly for a book on Christian education, we have there the Bible's first reference to a "teacher:" Tubal-Cain was an instructor in industrial arts (v.22). Most teachers do not realize that Tubal-Cain was the founding father of their profession!

This initial development of the Dominion Mandate is described in the context of the first reference to "city," and it is in the same context that the first teacher appears. Man was supposed to move out from the Garden, subdue the wilderness, and build a city. That's where the story ends in Revelation—the city of God established on earth. The tragedy is that man, from the onset of human sin, determined to rebelliously build his own city, using his learning and acquired skills to make a name for himself (Genesis 4:17; 11:4). Rather than giving weight to God's honor, man chose to elevate his own reputation. God's plan was for a city that reflected His glory (Revelation 21:11).

While man has attempted to hijack God's original purposes to his own ends, the fact remains: we have been made to rule, and we are born city-builders. Everybody is involved in building one city or another. Education is an expression of this life of the city. Christian education seeks to see this city life unfold in the context of subduing the earth for God's glory rather than for man's.

The City rather than the Temple

The motif of "city" is one of the Bible's important recurring themes. The Bible can be read as *A Tale of Two Cities*, to borrow Dickens' title. Both cities appear repeatedly from Genesis to Revelation. Abraham waits for a city whose builder and architect is God, while Cain and his descendents pioneer the building of Babylon whose destruction in Revelation is related to the fulfillment of the New Jerusalem. Augustine called these the city of man and the city of God. But what is the significance of a city?

The Old Testament speaks often of the City of God, and in the New Testament Jesus continues to speak of the church as a "city set on a hill." Roderick Campbell helpfully suggests that, "In New Covenant terminology, 'temple' means the covenanted worshipping community, while 'city' means the same community in all its other varied activities."[3] This observation recognizes that there is more to the Christian life than attending worship services. Certainly worship is a fundamental part of our lives, and the metaphor of "temple" describes that facet. But what we do on Monday morning is as important to the Lord as what we do on Sunday morning; most of God's people spend much more of their lives in the context of "city" than "temple." This is the way that God designed us.

It is on Monday mornings, in our lives as city-dwellers, that we pursue the creation mandate to subdue the earth to God's glory. It is in the context of the city that Jesus told us that our good deeds will shine out to the glory of God (Matthew 5:14-16). We think of glorifying God in a worship service in the "temple" on Sunday; Jesus spoke of glorifying God in the "city" on Monday.

The city represents all the varied activities that make up human life in community. A city is much more than a geographical location or a conglomeration of buildings. In the city we cooperate together in business, health care, education, leisure, raising families, earning a living, building houses, trading, manufacturing, media, politics, law and order, and a thousand other such pursuits. The city reflects the subduing of the barren wilderness, filling it instead with the development of civilization. All of us, whether our calling is to fix broken cars, to wash dishes, to provide employment, or to care for the sick, contribute to that Dominion Mandate. This mandate determines the scope of our curriculum.

Training City-dwellers

With this in mind, we see that the purpose of Christian education is to raise and train effective city-dwellers, not merely participating temple-dwellers. The church has been good at developing a curriculum for the temple: we are able to train our young people in how to read their Bibles, how to pray, how to sing spiritual songs, and we understand the need to teach basic doctrines as well as maturing character qualities in the process of sanctification. However, we have devoted considerably less attention to a specifically Christian approach to the concerns of city-dwellers. If all we do is to be to the glory of God, we surely need to know how to raise families, manage our finances, work diligently, engage in research, govern wisely, and trade fairly—all to the glory of God. The world does all these things very effectively, but to a different end. Rather than seeking God's glory, the goal for the world's citizens is summed up in the Babylonian desire: "to make a name for [themselves]" (Genesis 11:4).

It is perhaps against this background of an alternative model of city-building that Jesus says to his followers that they are to be a "...*city that is set on a hill*" (Matthew 5:14). It is there that we are to "let our light so shine before men so that they see [our] good works and glorify [our] Father in heaven." It is in our *city* works that God is to be glorified; the world rarely sees what we do behind the closed doors of the temple.

The word translated here as city is *polis* in the original Greek text, the word from which we derive our word "politics." The church is supposed to be a body politic! We are supposed to be an exalted demonstration to the world of how political life should work in a world that has now been invaded by the redemptive work of Christ. We should be a living example of the life of a civilized community when Jesus has removed the distortions created by the Fall.

When the world looks at the church, it thinks of us primarily as a kind of temple. We have a reputation for being able to preach sermons, run prayer meetings, and take up offerings. If they want to know how to do those things better they might come to us to ask for advice. But actually they have little interest in being able to do those things. Maybe they should want to, but they don't. But they do want to know how to raise their families better, how to manage their finances, how to run their businesses. In other words, they are desperately looking for a city set on a hill with some light to shine into these daily realities. But all they see is a temple. If they could see our good works as enlightened city dwellers they really might say "Wow! God has some amazing insights about how to live!"

While the church has focused on its calling to be a temple, it has neglected the emphasis that the Scriptures place on the idea of "the city of the Lord." This is an idea that recurs throughout the Bible and which is central in the ultimate consummation of human history. God's redemptive purposes on earth are finally fulfilled in the earthly manifestation of the heavenly city. The New Jerusalem comes down from heaven. That is to say, somewhat surprisingly, the Book of Revelation does not end with heaven, but with earth, and in particular with the city of heavenly origin being established on earth. What is more, the description we have there is actually of a city that no longer has need for a temple (Revelation 21:22), for the glory of God is finally all-pervasive, filling all of life, not merely the religious segments.

No Secular /Sacred Divide

Here in Revelation, we see the ultimate destruction of the great divide between the secular and the spiritual. One of the major demonic deceptions of history has been to persuade God's people that such a distinction exists. The devil is happy to let us be as "spiritual" as we like, just as long as it doesn't affect our everyday life. Correspondingly human empires from ancient Rome to modern Canada are happy for us to be as spiritual as we like, just as long as we do not take our "personal" religion out of the private realm into the public sphere. They are happy for us to be a temple as long as we leave the city to them. Education has been considered as part of city life; the world still wants to control that. We, in turn, have been persuaded that "politics is a dirty business" so we even feel self-righteous in having nothing to do with it. After all, are we not exhorted to "Come out and be separate"?

But being separate does not mean leaving the city to hide in the temple. It means recognizing that the way that the world builds the city is alien to God's way. We should be quite separate and distinct, not in having nothing to do with the city, but in being involved in an entirely different kind of city building. This includes an entirely different kind of education. Our city building, like the New Jerusalem, is to come down from heaven. It is to be God's will being "done on earth as it is in heaven" as opposed to the earthly Babylon, which defiantly reaches up toward heaven, built on human will seeking to "make a name for ourselves." Being separate means having an entirely different set of blueprints for building an entirely different city—a city "...*whose builder and maker is God*" (Hebrews 11:10) —but a city nonetheless. In other words, our task in Christian education is to train distinctly Christian citizens, not merely faithful members of church congregations. In that task we must recognize that true spirituality has to do with being led by the Spirit to do the will of God in all of life.

Sadly, we are still influenced by the Platonic separation of life into secular and sacred categories. The temple is seen as spiritual, and the city is seen as secular. As Christian Overman points out, our thinking in many areas reflects this false dichotomy.[4] We read *The Bible and Black Beauty*, regarding one as a sacred book, the other as a secular one. We listen to a violinist play two pieces: "How Great Thou Art" and Beethoven's "Sonata in C Minor," calling one a sacred piece and the other secular. We look at two paintings: one depicts the Last Supper and the other an elderly farmer standing with his wife and holding a pitchfork in his hand. We think of one as sacred and the other as secular. And then, of course, we think of a preacher's work as sacred while a factory worker's labor is regarded as secular.

But the biblical idea of a city opposes this dichotomy. The farmer and the factory worker may be both doing God's work. The novelist and the musician can glorify God in the beauty of their work despite the absence of religious words. The contrast is not between sacred and secular—as if God's realm comprises things like the Bible, "How Great Thou Art," a painting of the Last Supper, and the labors of a preacher, whereas *Black Beauty*, a Beethoven sonata, a portrait of a farmer, and the efforts of a factory worker, because they do not deal with "sacred" subjects, somehow belong to a lower realm. Rather, there are two kinds of cities: work, literature, music, etc. done to God's glory—and the same things done to man's glory.

Overman helpfully describes the false and true way of making distinctions about what is truly spiritual in the following way[5]:

Figure 1: The False Dichotomy

SACRED

Things pertaining to the spiritual,

eternal and unchanging upper realm of God

in heaven

SECULAR

Things pertaining to the physical,

temporal, and changing lower realm of man

on earth

The view of Beethoven's violin sonata as being secular and the instrumental version of "How Great Thou Art" being spiritual follows the thinking illustrated in Figure 1. Of course we are not saying there are no distinctions to be drawn in matters of art or work. But a better way of understanding the distinction is as illustrated in Figure 2:

Figure 2: The True Contrast

THE CITY OF MAN		THE CITY OF GOD
	Church	
	School	
	Art	
	Home	
Done in	Music	Done in
Conflict	Literature	Harmony
With	Science	With
God's	Sport	God's
Design	Business	Design
	Work	
	Law	
	Agriculture	
	Medicine	

In this view, everything can be done to either one goal or the other: God's glory or man's glory. It is too simplistic to say that church work is spiritual and factory work is secular. It is possible for church to be part of the city of man—to go through all those religious activities seeking the glory and honor of man. Preachers can be building their own reputation and career, in which case their activity is part of the city of man rather than the city of God. A church can be built according to God's design or it can be in conflict with God's design as it reflects human desires. But a business, or a home, or a school, or an orchestra, or a farm can be built as part of the city of God, operating according to God's design and aimed at serving God's glory.

The Bible does not speak of secular things, only of worldly things. Politics, for example, only becomes worldly when it functions independently of God's design. But it can be truly spiritual when that political activity is in harmony with God's thoughts. Our task in Christian education is to seek to understand God's thoughts on every subject and to bring every discipline into captivity to His thoughts. We have to take education out of the city of man and see how it can best be pursued in the context of the city of God. And we have to see its goal as being the preparation of a generation of city-dwellers.

ENDNOTES

1. Jay Adams: Back to the Blackboard—Design for a biblical Christian School (Phillipsburg: Presbyterian & Reformed Publishing; 1982) p.23

2. D.J.Smethwick: Teachers, curriculum, control (Nehemiah Institute; 1998) p.5

3. Roderick Campbell: Israel and the New Covenant (Philadelphia: Presbyterian & Reformed Publishing; 1954) p.142

4. Christian Overman: Assumptions that Affect our Lives (Chatsworth CA: Mich 6:8; 1996) p.176

5. ibid p.181

Chapter 4

The City of Man and the City of God

Since Adam was created, man has been wired to build. It was intended to be that way, but with the distortion of sin, what he has built and the way in which he has built have radically deviated from the original divine commission.

Cain was Adam's first biological descendant. He is also the prototype of all of Adam's descendants apart from the redemptive work of Christ. Paul is clear: we are all either in Adam or in Christ. Cain was the one who first revealed the way that sons of Adam live, immortalized in his city-building venture. This was specifically designed as a means to perpetuate his dynasty, as seen in his decision to name his city after his son (Genesis 4:17). Genesis 11:4 says he was "...*making a name for himself.*" But the Bible is clear that this city was far more than a collection of buildings in a geographical location. It was the context in which the process we call "civilization" was begun.

God had actually forbidden Cain to settle down. He condemned Cain to being a wandering fugitive after he murdered his brother. God's plan was that city-building would be the domain of His Son, the new Adam.

But Cain declared that this punishment was "...*greater than [he] could bear*" (Genesis 4:13). The desire in him to build was a fire burning with the passion of the purposes for which God had originally created man, now further fuelled by his own sinful determination to make his own life count. The city that he built was constructed in the attitude of going "...*out from the presence of the LORD*" (Genesis 4:16). And it was in this environment of separation from the Lord that new forms of agriculture were developed, novel housing arrangements emerged, innovative industrial arts appeared, and musical expression began to flourish in new and diverse ways (Genesis 4:20-22). In other words, culture blossomed—apart from God.

What are we to make of the fact that this emerging culture (including education—the first "teacher") is described as the fruit of a godless city? At first glance we see that these exciting new developments in the process of civilization emerged in the context of man's rebellion. Do we conclude that as Christians we should therefore withdraw from all cultural involvement, shunning it as an expression of man's alienation from God acted out in a forbidden city life? This represents the posture of many well-meaning Christians. They are rightly focussed on heaven, but wrongly content to let the devil have the world, seeking to have as little as possible to do with what happens in city life down here.

But it would be wrong to assume that the developments recorded in the cultural progress of Cain's descendents imply that these activities have their *origins* in sinful man's rebellion. All of those developments listed, plus many more, may also be seen in the New Jerusalem and in God's plans to build His city. The way in which they occurred in the city of man has been a gross distortion of God's plan, but these distortions are nonetheless distortions of God's original and still valid purposes for city life.

A balanced understanding avoids two dangers at opposite poles. Christians tend to fall prey to one or other of these. On the one hand we must not *over-estimate* the work of the enemy: cultural progress in the world is not the creation of the kingdom of darkness. On the other hand, we should not *under-estimate* the work of the enemy: cultural progress has been significantly hijacked by the kingdom of darkness to serve its ends. We shall consider these dangers by reference to one of the dimensions of cultural progress recorded in Cain's city: music. We shall then explore more generally the implications of this for Christian education committed to training godly citizens to impact the culture of this present world.

Culture is not the Creation of the Kingdom of Darkness

Too often, Christians fear culture as if it were nothing but a manifestation of the kingdom of darkness. They try to hide from the city in the isolation of the temple. Some parents pursue Christian education as an expression of this separatist mindset: they want their children isolated from the life of the city and are suspicious of every facet of cultural development.

Consider the implications of this line of thought in the realm of music. If it were true that music was born in Cain's city, then cultural isolation might be a reasonable reaction. Does it not say in Genesis 4:21 that Cain's descendant Jubal was the "...*father of all who play the harp and flute*"? Is not this the first reference to any form of music as we read the Bible? The question is sometimes asked, "Why should the devil have all the good music?" If this reading of Genesis 4 is accurate, then the answer to that question must be that he has all the good music because music was born in a culture of rebellion, in separation from the life of God.

Actually, music did not originate in Cain's city. While this may be the first reference to music in the Bible, the Bible is also clear that music goes back much further. It is, after all, the very atmosphere of heaven where God had existed before time began. But even in human terms, music predates Cain. We find this in a later passage in the Bible (Ezekiel 28), though it is a passage that has frequently been misunderstood. While Ezekiel was written after Genesis, here it speaks of a time prior to Genesis 4. The music of heaven was part of what God put into man at creation.

At the Fall, the music of heaven was replaced by, or at least adulterated by, the music of hell. But we do get a glimpse of the unspoiled beginnings in Ezekiel 28:11-19. This is an oracle against the king of Tyre, a powerful world leader who got "too big for his boots" and started acting tyrannically as he began to think of himself as a god. He was another of those rebellious city-builders, building a civilization to make a name for himself. Some have seen this whole chapter as a description of satan (e.g. Ezekiel 28:2a), but few reputable Bible scholars defend that view. In fact, it is clear that this is a *man* being spoken of here (Ezekiel 28:2.b). The most likely interpretation is that Ezekiel sees in the king of Tyre a man who repeated all over again the tragedy of Adam: a representative man (a king) who started out in the most perfect of surroundings with everything going for him, until he fell (Ezekiel 28:11-15). As such, this king of Tyre is an example of the fallen state of man.

In that context, note what is said in Ezekiel 28:12,13 about him (and thus about us as human beings):

* *"You were the **SEAL** of perfection."* A seal is an imprint made from an original: the hallmark of the creator was stamped in the creature. Man was made in the image of God.

* *"You were the seal of **PERFECTION**."* The perfection that was imprinted in the seal is described as *wisdom*, which includes the realm of the intellect and character, and *beauty*, which encompasses the realm of art. The beauty of heaven was stamped into man's artistic endeavors (God's will being done on earth, in art, as it is in heaven). This is part of what it means to "worship the Lord in the beauty of holiness:" it is to worship with the perfect beauty that reflects the very life of heaven which is holy, that is to say, totally separate from anything of a contaminated world. The word "perfection" here could literally be translated "symmetry," which, incidentally, sets this apart as one of the key criteria by which art is to be judged: form and structure are vital to good art.

* *"The service [of music—timbrels and pipes] was prepared IN YOU at creation."* This is Matthew Henry's translation of Ezekial 28:13. Music was put into man at creation as a means of facilitating worship. This, then, is the source of all true music and all genuine worship. Tragically, when the beauty of all that God had placed in man was taken over by man's dreadful urge to make a name for himself, that beauty was thrown down. As with all the other facets of man's created genius that were intended to be used to God's glory, music became adulterated in the vain attempt to glorify man apart from God.

So, music did not originate in Cain's city—it originated in heaven. As one aspect of culture, music is part of "city life." God's intent for city life was always that it would "come down from heaven" as it ultimately does in its final consummation in Revelation 21,22. Jesus urged us to pray that the Kingdom would come. That prayerful desire for the coming of the Kingdom has a futuristic component, but it is also seen in the ongoing reality of God's will "being done on earth as it is in heaven." In the realm of music, that means that the Kingdom comes when music is done on earth the way that it is being done in heaven.

Cain's descendants did not give birth to music as some unprecedented phenomenon. But they did develop its potential in their own man-glorifying city. They came up with novel ways to distort something from its beautiful, intended function of engaging man's pleasure in the glory of God, into an expression of man's autonomous desire to build for himself. Don't give the devil too much credit: good music does not originate in his kingdom, nor does any other part of the Dominion Mandate to make the world beautiful and productive to the glory of God. The city was God's idea, and Christians need to live there!

Consequently, Christian education must not be afraid of exploring every facet of cultural richness. We dare not withdraw into our religious ghetto assuming that all that is around us in city life is the devil's idea. Certainly culture as we see it is a distortion of God's purpose for a gloriously stimulating life surrounded by the beauty of art and music, sumptuously fed by wonderful gastronomic possibilities, and assisted by innovative technological advances in every area of our life. But culture and civilization are not the devil's brainwave. All he has done is spoil God's plan. The task of Christian education is to reclaim the city for God's glory.

Culture has been Hijacked by the Kingdom of Darkness

Some Christians step back from all cultural involvement in fear, somehow believing this to be the domain of the kingdom of darkness. They prefer to remain in holy isolation until they are transported to their heavenly home. But other Christians feel too much at home down here! Their danger is in minimizing the implications of the fact that culture, as we know it, has come down to us largely through Cain's descendants. To a large degree, culture is an expression of the kingdom of man; there is very little evidence of God's will being done on earth as is in heaven.

Man has taken the cultural mandate and has been in the process of subduing the earth for thousands of years. But he has not been stewarding the created order to the glory of God; he has been laying claim to it for his own ends. The result is as clear in ecological devastation as it is in musical anarchy. We will briefly continue to pursue this in our example of the realm of music.

The kingdom of God has to do with God's will being done on earth as it is in heaven. The criterion of *good* music is that it is the music of heaven. His will concerning music is doing music on earth in the way that it is done in heaven. Think about that for a moment in relation to worship. Our worship is not to emerge out of the styles and tastes of the culture: it is to be an expression of what is going on in heaven. The Bible is clear: heaven is to be the pattern for all earthly worship. Hebrews 8:1-5 and 9:23,24 are clear: our worship structures on earth are copies of the pattern established in heaven and revealed "on the mountain." The mountain was the place where God revealed his will to man; for us that is in the Word. If you really want to get hold of the latest worship CD to see what's hot in the worship world, that's where we should go: worship live in heaven! I wonder what that sounds like! I wonder how important the PA system is? I wonder if they all sit in rows so they can see the screen displaying the words from the overhead projector! I wonder if there is a band on stage or an organ in the loft? I wonder if there is a worship leader—or is that title reserved only for the Holy Spirit? These are actually much more important questions for modern churches wrestling with worship styles than attempts to be relevant to a culture hell-bent on destruction.

In the current phenomenon of the worship industry we see modern Christians' tragic error of underestimating the significance of the role of the kingdom of darkness in the development of culture. It is not inaccurate to speak of worship as an "industry" in our day: 40% of the North American music business is now from sales of so-called Christian music, and most labels, even those marketing worship CD's are owned and run for profit by non-Christians. Similarly, some significant Christian publishing houses are owned by anti-Christian tycoons, including one owned by Rupert Murdoch whose "Sun" newspaper in the U.K. is best known for its regular nude photos on page three. Integrity Hosanna is operated by a public company listed on the New York Stock Exchange, operated for the profit of its shareholders. "Worship" songs may make their writers instant millionaires. For whom is this music being written?

We blindly assume that God is excited about modern worship trends. We imagine He must have been dreadfully bored by centuries of having nothing to listen to other than dull hymns and occasional snatches of Bach. But this idea is perhaps more a reflection of the fact that we would have been bored by a diet of such worship music. Having created God in our own image (in our imaginations), we assume He is bored when we are bored. This reversion is actually an expression of our desire that what is done on earth would be done in heaven. Our prayer is that our will will be permanently done in heaven as it is on earth. We project our taste in music and imagine that eternity will now "rock on" forever because, fortunately, the guitar and drums have been incorporated into worship styles just in the nick of time. If history had ended before the twentieth century, God and we would have been stuck with nothing more exciting than harps and organs for ever. One internationally known charismatic leader even preached that God had to raise up the Beatles in order to make it possible for the church to begin to worship properly.

The tragedy is that modern Christian music styles are often a poor imitation of what the world was doing a few years earlier. We have become followers and imitators of the city of man, not realizing that so many cultural developments actually reflect the process indicated in Genesis 4, where Cain and his descendants took the divinely implanted gifts and motivations for the Dominion Mandate and misused them to build a civilization to the glory of man.

We should not be following the world. The world has made a dreadful mess of managing the earth and has built civilizations that have had a catastrophic effect on millions of people created in God's image. We have abused the power that He has given to us.

So, while Christian education must not shy away from cultural engagement, neither must it be enamored with all that is going on around it. Music, like all other expressions of culture, is vitally important. But our task is not to perpetrate the civilization of man apart from God. Our task is to re-think music. Rather than being mindless followers of fashion, we are to rediscover God's purpose in this and every other area of city life. Our conclusions should be radically different.

Civilization: Cultural Progression, Regression, or Digression?

What is true of music is true of every dimension of the cultural mandate. Each contains its own horror stories of what man has done. We have made huge progress in the realm of agriculture, but have we treated either the land or the hungry as God intended? We have taken huge strides in scientific research, but as well as developing nuclear power as an energy source, we have developed it as a weapon of mass destruction. We have multiplied our talents and generated huge wealth, as we were intended to. But we have done so in ways that often were illegal or exploitative and for ends that were ungodly. We have developed incredible medical techniques, but we have used them to kill as well as to heal, to avoid the consequences of sinful sexuality as well as to promote life.

Everything around us is tainted to a significant degree, and we live in the city of man. It is inevitable that we live in the city of man, but all too often we are comfortable there, adopting unquestioningly the mindset, worldview, and habit patterns of Cain's descendants apart from God. Even in our Christian schools we teach the curriculum of the city of man, perhaps with a few Bible verses added and certainly taught by sincere Christian staff. But the tools of dominion have been in the hands of the kingdom of darkness for so long that we have forgotten to ask, "How can your will be done on earth as it is in heaven?"

We will only be able to ask such a fundamental question when we learn to be deeply suspicious of all that happens in the city of man. When Dr J.I. Packer addressed Regent College's 23rd Annual Convocation, he charged the graduates to develop such a suspicion. He challenged our assumption that, because the church has been actively involved in the task of Christianizing culture for centuries, then it follows that our current culture is essentially Christian. He suggests that on this basis we have become largely conformist. We only expect to be cultural non-conformists in exceptional circumstances (such as when we face the abortion industry or the pornography empires or the drug trade). But, argues Packer:

> Instead of taking for granted that we are called to deviate from the conventional only on [such] specific issues, [...] we must get it into our heads that we are called to be different consistently and

systematically. As Christ's disciples, we march to the beat of a different drummer. Intellectually and imaginatively we must absorb the fact that our calling as Christians means becoming God's alternative society. Instead of thoughtlessly going with the world except when we have particular reason not to, we should see ourselves as summoned to think out from scratch the Christian way to approach everything, and only go along with the world when we have particular Christian and biblical reasons for doing so.

In other words, the world's way, the city of man, is a Babylon from which we should depart. We have to start again. Music must be rethought, and the world's approach to music must be pressed through a biblical grid. Science practiced the way it is in the world must be regarded with suspicion, simply because it is developed in a context of human autonomy and rebellion. Schools and hospitals, police stations and businesses, factories and farms—they all look different in the city of God. *"Come out from among them and be separate"* (2 Corinthians 6:17) means far more than not watching X-rated movies. It is "Babylon" from which we are to come out (Revelation 18:4), a city of trading and merchants, of wealth and art, of resources and agriculture, all designed to satisfy the wants and needs of man in every part of his life (Rev 18:6-16). It is an all-pervasive approach to life and the human condition that is doomed and which must be replaced by God's way of living.

The City of God

As we have stated, "An illuminated city is Jesus' model for the light of the kingdom. Our task is to shed the light of God's Word on every facet of life—personal, domestic, social, political, and economic. Our message must have relevance to society as much as to the Church. Our mandate is to shine out to show the world how every area of life should be lived under the government of God, as revealed in the Word of God."[1]

Education is one of the most vital areas of city life. It is here that we learn how to use the tools of dominion that God has placed in our hands. What we do with those tools will largely be determined by the nature of those who carry influence in the realm of education. It is they who will teach the next generation how to live.

Just over a hundred years ago, Christians began to evacuate the city. This, as we will consider in Part Six, was in many ways due to novel ideas of eschatology that were emerging in the nineteenth century, views which now dominate much Christian thinking. It was an eschatology that put off all hope of victory until the after-life. This has been called "an eschatology of ship-wreck." Instead of trying to build anything to rival the sinking ship of humanism, the cry has been to take to the lifeboats. The only hope is the hope of the life vest: personal salvation for the few who will make it to the far shore while the world is left to sink. "We are beginning to pay the price for that philosophy. The defeatist vision which led Christians to withdraw from the world has meant that as we have left the battlefield, the humanists have been winning by default. They now hold most of the key positions."[2]

But defeatism and escapism have not always characterized the church of Jesus Christ. When the Pilgrims arrived in North America, it is true that on one level they were seeking to escape—to come out from the tyranny of what they saw as the city of man, the human expression of the kingdom of darkness in the European culture that they were leaving. But their goal was neither negative nor escapist. As John Winthrop sat aboard the *Arabella* just prior to landing in the New World, he wrote about the vision that lay before them:

> Thus stands the cause between God and us: we are entered into covenant with Him for this work[…] We shall surely find that the God of Israel is among us, when ten of us shall be able to resist a thousand of our enemies, when He shall make us a praise and glory, that men of succeeding generations shall say, 'The Lord make us like that of New England.' For we must consider that we shall be as a City upon a Hill.[3]

With this vision before them, the Pilgrims set about building far more than religious edifices. Certainly, they quickly constructed church buildings in their communities. But their goal was to build whole societies that were built on biblical foundations. Their dream was to see a tangible expression of the kingdom of God in the New World that the Lord had opened up for them.

Jesus' Kingdom: on Earth as it is in Heaven

What does this Puritan vision have to do with Christian education? Here is our example of godly men and women who believed that God's glory would be revealed to the world in all of life if that life were lived in obedience to his ways. It is at least as important to train young people to be godly citizens as it is to train them to be faithful church members. It is vital to explore the numerous tasks that comprise the venture of city-building. These tasks must be pursued in ways that both honor God's blueprints for the city of which He is the architect and builder and are directed toward His glory rather than our own aggrandizement.

Jesus is God's primary city builder. It is a mistake to think that Jesus was only interested in what we characterize as the spiritual dimension of life. Certainly He taught people how to do such things as pray. But His interest was in whole people and all of life. He declared that there was a revelation of the in-breaking of the new Kingdom in the miracles He performed. Many of these miracles revealed His deep commitment to issues of physical and material life as well as to addressing spiritual problems. Indeed His miracles, in one sense, reflect His own pursuit of the mandate given to man to bring the whole created order into subjection to the glory of God.

Jay Adams describes the relation between the Dominion Mandate and the science curriculum in a Christian school. He draws our attention to the fact that Jesus, in His miracles, demonstrated God's original intention for mankind's ruling role.[4] Jesus took authority over creation. He dealt with disease and sickness without necessarily making physical healing contingent on spiritual renewal in those He ministered to. He provided food and drink, as well as spiritual refreshment, by His mastery over the physical world. As Willard puts it, He "knew how to transform the molecular structure of water to make it wine. That knowledge also allowed him to take a few pieces of bread and some little fish and feed thousands of people."[5] Jesus knew how to solve problems of human hunger (feeding 5000), poverty (finding cash in a fish's mouth!), and ineffectual work (instructing the fishermen to put their nets over the other side). He was able to suspend gravity (walk on water), interrupt weather patterns and control wind and water (stilling the storm), and eliminate unfruitful trees without saw or axe. Just this limited list of some of Jesus' miracles immediately gives us a clear example of the legitimate areas of human endeavor.

Our access to the supernatural realm of miracles may be rather more limited than Jesus'. But the legitimacy of pursuing the same goals through "scientific" means is seen in the fact that Jesus clearly saw that subduing the created order was part of his job description as the Perfect Man, the new Adam who succeeded where the first Adam had failed. Our methods may be different, but these are some of the areas in which we, as followers of Christ, are to take dominion.

However, in saying that we may pursue such goals as subduing sickness, hunger, and poverty, or limiting the ravages of powerful storms by scientific means, we should not make the mistake of thinking that we are limited to merely "natural" methods. It is foolish to approach science as if the universe were a closed system of natural laws. Any Christian approach to science must include the dynamic of prayer that can instantly and inexplicably change the outcome of the most controlled laboratory experiment. Our task is to use all the means that God has put in our hands to bring His government into the world; our students need to be trained to pray for the sick and to engage in medical research as complementary facets of the same Dominion Mandate.

Jesus' Example: Spiritual, Earthly Rule

The Bible explicitly states that Jesus is to be our example as a ruler. Man was made to rule in Genesis, but in the Fall he forfeited that privilege. Satan became the prince of this world, though we should note that it was man's place of government that he usurped; he never unseated God from His throne, only man from his. Consequently, man barely resembles God's original intention.

The writer to the Hebrews commented on this dilemma as he quoted from Psalm 8. "*What is man?*" the psalmist had asked. In principle he had been "*...set over the works of [God's] hands;*" God had "*...put all things in subjection under his feet.*" However, as Hebrews says, "*But now we do not see all things put under him;*" the psalmist's description of man as ruler seems to bear little relation to the reality around us. Thankfully this is not the end of the story: "*But we see Jesus [...]crowned with glory and honor,*" and He is now in the process of "*...bringing many sons to glory*" (Hebrews 2:6-10). Jesus is our model of ruling, the Man who rules as man was originally intended to rule, and the one who is leading us back to the place which we lost in Adam.

Jesus' rule is clearly a spiritual rule (in that His power was from above), but it is exercised on earth over all of creation, not merely so-called "spiritual" realities. From this we conclude that Christian schools should not simply be junior Bible Colleges, but institutions committed to the task of training young people to fulfill every aspect of Christ's multi-faceted rule.

As Jesus' miracles suggest, science is an example of that rule. Since the city of God is fundamentally different from the city of man, science cannot be taught in the same way in education that is truly Christian as it is in secular schools. Science must be built on the foundation of the God who is personally involved in all the affairs of men, the God who causes the wind to blow by His personal word rather than by blind laws of nature (e.g. Psalm 147:15-18). It must also be taught in the context of wisdom as well as knowledge, with a deep concern for what we do with our knowledge in a commitment to devote all our energy and activity to the glory of God. Science must have as its goal the glory of God. But for both Adam and Jesus, science reflects part of man's appropriate dominion of the created order, whether in naming animals or in harnessing the power of the wind.

Our curriculum in Christian education encompasses far more than the music and science that we have referred to in this chapter. For God's will to be done as it is in heaven, each subject that is taught should be seen as part of the training necessary to enable students to take their place in ruling that microcosm of the created order in which they have been called. There is no higher calling than to take one's place in doing the "...*good works which God prepared beforehand*" for us to walk in (Ephesians 2:10)—good works in the city set on the hill, works that men will see and which will lead them to glorify God. There is no greater privilege than preparing young people for life, equipping them for works of service—works of service as city-dwellers; service in which it is just as spiritual to be a plumber as to be a preacher if that plumbing is done to the glory of God.

ENDNOTES

1. Brian Watts: The Treasure in the Field—Digging to discover the Kingdom of God (Upper Hutt NZ; Spirit of Truth; 1995) p.110f

2. ibid p.120

3. "Winthrop Papers": Quoted by Marshall & Manuel: The Light and the Glory (Old Tappan NJ: Fleming H Revell; 1977) p.161f

4. Jay Adams: Back to the Blackboard—Design for a biblical Christian School (Phillipsburg: Presbyterian & Reformed Publishing; 1982) p.40ff

5. Dallas Willard: The Divine Conspiracy (San Fransisco: HarperCollins; 1998) p.94f

Part 3

The Scope of our Curriculum:

Christian Education Serves the Whole Child,
not Just Academics

Chapter 5

Heads and Hearts

The word curriculum means "course." We usually think of it as a course of study in some academic discipline, but in its Latin roots, the word referred to a race course rather than a study course. This, of course (pun intended!), opens up a lot of biblical allusions. Life is thought of as running a race; Paul's final letter describes his satisfaction at having completed the course (2 Timothy 4:7).

As Christian parents consider the appropriate education for their children, they must have a broad view of curriculum. There is a subtle danger in young people feeling that they have completed the course when they pass a final exam. They may have acquired a body of knowledge (though most are happy to forget it as soon as the exam results are published), but, as Paul tells us in 1 Corinthians 8:1, knowledge of this sort tends to puff up. The real course is the race of life that God has mapped out for each child. A truly Christian education is geared at preparing young people to run the whole race. And that requires a lot more than academics.

It is a startling fact that there is a long list of highly educated people who are largely responsible for perpetrating the atrocities that have filled human history in the last hundred years. Clearly the solution to the world's problems does not simply lie with education! Education may have a significant role to play, but it must be kept in mind that education *may* only serve to cultivate more sophisticated sinners, giving them more tools with which to pursue their sinfulness.

Advancing the intellectual life of students without a corresponding development of their moral character may prove highly detrimental. Knowledge apart from wisdom is a recipe for disaster. Christian education must pursue character training as well as academic excellence. But we should not separate those two tasks as if they stand independently.

Academic subjects must not exist in a vacuum unrelated to real life. The courses we teach in Christian schools and home-schooling programs must be integrated with the development of our students' character and pursued with a view to application in real life to the glory of God. This begins with appreciating that we must not limit our role to the purely academic realm. The cerebral world of facts, information, and ideas cannot be isolated from the world of practical affairs. The goal is to teach children, not to teach information.

Teachers are tempted to think of their subject matter as all-important. That's what they spend their time preparing. The lesson plan in the day book focuses on the amount of material to be covered, the information to be imparted. A good lesson is assumed to be one in which we get through all the notes. A bad lesson is one in which we had intended to get from page 67 in the text book right through to the end of the chapter, but we got distracted and will have to come back to the last five pages in the next class. We feel like we're getting behind. It's all about getting through the material on schedule because final exams are looming.

But Jesus' teaching model is a relational rather than an informational model. He chose his students with the primary goal of being with them (Mark 3:14). He was interested in them as people. He did not see them as "vessels arranged in order, ready to have imperial gallons of facts poured into them until they were full to the brim," as Charles Dickens described the prevalent teachers' mindset of his day.

Facts, Facts, Facts!

Dickens' description of students as pots lined up waiting to be filled with facts is found in his novel *Hard Times*. In this novel, Dickens caricatures and parodies the educational philosophy of the enlightenment era, in which human nature is seen to be purely rational. One of the central characters is Thomas Gradgrind, whose speech to a group of students opens the book:

Now what I want is Facts. Teach these boys and girls nothing but Facts. Facts alone are wanted in life. Plant nothing else, and root out everything else. You can form the minds of reasoning animals on facts; nothing else will ever be of service to them. This is the principle on which I bring up my own children, and this is the principle on which I bring up these children. Stick to Facts, sir!

Thomas Gradgrind is not an unkind man; in many ways he is a genuinely loving father and a kind benefactor. But his philosophy of education is summed up in his name, a carefully contrived name that Dickens uses to make his point. Sadly, the name reflects the way that many students in our day feel about their years in school: the grind toward grad. For Gradgrind, education was all about the grind to understand the facts.

But as the novel unfolds, Gradgrind's well-intentioned ideals disintegrate in the hard times that befall his loved ones as a direct result of his educational philosophy. In particular, his daughter Louisa meets with great sadness, and when she finally returns to the room where she had been a studious child, Gradgrind begins to see the emptiness of his worldview:

Some persons hold," he pursued, still hesitating, "that there is a wisdom of the Head, and that there is a wisdom of the Heart. I have not supposed so; but, as I have said, I mistrust myself now. I have supposed the head to be all-sufficient; how can I venture this morning to say it is! If that other kind of wisdom should be what I have neglected, and should be the instinct that is wanted, Louisa…"
He suggested it very doubtfully as if he were half unwilling to admit it even now.

Some of us were raised in schools not too different from Dickens' parody. Education was all about facts. History was about dates. Mathematics was about multiplication tables. Students were seen as heads to be filled, not people to be developed and trained. Pupils were considered, in Gradgrind's phrase, as "reasoning animals." Education was geared to that rational capacity.

Of course, in this post-modern era, rationality is no longer in vogue. It would seem that, to use Gradgrind's terminology, the wisdom of the head has been entirely superceded by the wisdom of the heart. Charles Colson reports a contemporary education professor telling his class of future language arts teachers: "More important than content or thinking are the students' feelings. You are not there to feed them information, but to be sensitive to their need for positive reinforcement, for self esteem."[1] Has this professor rectified the problems Dickens identified? Surely he speaks as the mouthpiece for the transformed Gradgrind, the man who now sees that the key is in the wisdom of the heart.

Dickens would not have been so simplistic. Even in his diatribe against rationalism gone wild, he balances the character of Louisa with Sissy, a helpless orphan from the circus, whom Gradgrind takes into his own home and raises by his own system. Sissy, being from the circus, is a hopeless romantic, filled with "fancy." But while she represents all that is lacking in Gradgrind's system as a girl of the heart, it is also clear as the story unfolds that, if it had not been for the kindness and the education which she received, she too would have been lost, though for the opposite reasons. Her father, a man of the circus, an uneducated clown, a man of fancy rather than fact, was a hopeless drunk. Dickens was not advocating heart *instead of* head, but heart *and* head—education for whole people.

Teaching Children, not Teaching Information

Until recent times, a casual look at most schools would indicate that they children were primarily seen in terms of heads into which information is to be poured. As the pendulum has swung away from such a view, "traditional" schools have emerged, priding themselves on retaining this academic emphasis. But there is now a greater recognition that children need to be understood holistically. While we may be cautious in entirely embracing the postmodern rejection of rationalism, at the very least we rejoice that this opens up the opportunity to rediscover the biblical ideal of seeing people as whole people. We have suffered long enough under the dualistic approach of Greek philosophies which separated and idealized the realm of the intellect from other parts of man's being. When school was all about brains and intellects, we know who succeeded and who failed in that environment. It prepared a minority of students for university courses but left a majority ill-prepared for the other course: the race of life.

But have we gone far enough in this regard? Neil Postman points out that, while it is generally accepted that the whole child is far more than merely intellect, most curricula still do not reflect this understanding. He suggests that the way that teachers commonly isolate the realm of the intellect often results in certain important aspects of students as whole human beings going largely unnoticed. For example, he notes wryly, most curricula "do not seem to recognize the fact that boys are different from girls. This is exceedingly odd since almost everybody else has noticed differences."[2]

We know, of course, that boys are different from girls. They learn differently from girls. A school that wants to treat children as individuals and whole persons will develop teaching strategies that recognize that the heart of a boy is quite different than that of a girl. If curriculum is seen as a number of chapters in a text book that must be mastered, it is more likely that the girls in the class will rise to the challenge more effectively than the boys. But if curriculum is seen as preparing whole people for life, more diverse and creative ways must be found to complete the necessary training.

Sadly, school is becoming an increasingly feminized environment. This is not just because there are more female teachers, especially in the lower grades. Rather, the fact that girls consistently achieve higher grades probably reveals, not that girls are more intelligent than boys, but that the teaching methods, the learning strategies, and the grading processes are weighted in favor of that which is more natural to them.

This is not only a matter of gender distinction. The differences between boys and girls merely illustrate all kinds of differences that exist among any group of students sitting in a classroom. All kinds of distinctions make it inevitable that different people, as whole people, learn in different ways. If curriculum is seen as a fixed body of information that each student has to assimilate within the same time frame, there are bound to be some losers. But if, to bend a clichè, we have *courses for horses*, surely we should have courses for children—effective preparation for life so that each is equipped to run the race that is set before them.

Not Either/Or, but Both/And

Postmodernism's rejection of rationalism creates both a problem and an opportunity for Christianity. There's a great opportunity. The modernist era, in its rationalism, was hostile to religion. That's now over; people are talking about the heart, and people are open to the supernatural. But there's also a problem. Postmodernism is just as hostile to Christianity as modernism ever was. As Os Guinness puts it:

"Sometimes we will side with postmodernism against modernism. But we may just as often side with modernism against postmodernism. Like modernism, for example, Christians reject irrationalism. For Christians to join in the public flogging of the dying horse of modernism—thereby reinforcing the relativism and irrationalism of postmodernism [...]—is fatuous and ironic."[3]

Trends in modern education are moving away from focusing on the head and toward focusing on the heart. Healthy self-esteem is preferred to correct spelling. Many Christians are becoming concerned about the direction that public schools are taking and the philosophies and lifestyles they propagate. They are looking at alternatives within the growing Christians school movement and in home-schooling options. The search to rediscover academic excellence is becoming a priority.

The need to retain a focus on head-knowledge is urgent. In addition to serious research, anecdotal evidence abounds, suggesting that the graduates of the modern educational system are less informed about the most elementary facts. On the Tonight Show, Jay Leno did one of his customary "man-on-the-street interviews" and asked some young people questions about the Bible. When asked to name one of the Ten Commandments, one college-aged young woman replied, "Freedom of Speech?" Another was asked to complete the sentence, "Let he who is without sin..."; her response was "Have a good time?" A third was asked, "Who, according to the Bible, was eaten by a whale?" His confident answer was, "Pinocchio." But their general knowledge is no better than their Bible knowledge. Johnny can't read, we are told, and he has difficulty finding France on a map, too.

But an excessive emphasis on head knowledge is dangerous. For some, the determination to avoid the spirit of the age will create pressure to nostalgically search for the lost past. Some "Get back to basics" approaches to education fall into this trap as they seek to revive an emphasis on basic academic disciplines instead of the new-fangled subjectivity and relativism.

Parent beware! The desire to help little Johnny to pass his exams and do his sums properly is admirable. But it may take us back into Gradgrind territory: it may trap Johnny in a dungeon of information and facts with no preparation for life in the real world. Hopefully he might prove to be one of those fortunate students who can master a rigorously academic approach. Yet even then, his awareness of how much he knows may be part of his downfall in a moral universe where "knowledge puffs up," fooling educated men to think that they can solve problems by their own reason without reference to God.

We dare not fall back into the pitfalls of the philosophy of the enlightenment era. Those were not the "good old days" when students were viewed as nothing more than rational animals. But we must also be careful that we are not simply getting carried along on the wave of a postmodernist reaction to modernity. The wisdom of the head is still a vital part of the education process. Environmental sensitivity and enhanced self-esteem do not prepare students any better for the real world than a head full of nothing but facts and figures. Children must learn to think. Christian parents are looking for the best environment for their children to become thinkers. And in a world where more and more people *feel* rather than *think*, our students as thinkers will inevitably rise to the top of their chosen callings.

More than Facts

Gradgrind's protègè, the teacher being charged in his opening speech before a classroom of students in *Hard Times*, was Mr M'Choakumchild (another name invented by Dickens to convey a meaning). As his character is developed, we read of him: "If only he had learnt a little less, how infinitely better he might have taught much more." Our task in Christian education is to explore the realms of "much more" and "infinitely better." There is much more to teaching than subject matter, and there are infinitely better ways of training young people than appear in secular educational fads, be they the trendiest ones in our day or the older ones of Dickens' times.

That is because, as we have stated, Christian education starts with *who* you know, not *what* you know. Our students may not suffer if they leave school with fewer facts in their heads if they can integrate the knowledge they have acquired into a living relationship with the Lord and a desire to apply all that they are learning to His service.

As we contemplate curriculum, we must stop thinking of it as an abstract body of information to be passed on. In Dickens' novel, the educational system that he described purported to be a purely rational endeavor, revolving entirely around facts. Christian parents still seem to feel safe if education is reduced to just the facts. They believe that even non-Christian teachers can be trusted if they would only stick to teaching the facts. But inevitably a worldview is being advanced.

Dickens insists on this throughout *Hard Times*. The students in the novel are not only being given mountains of facts; they are also being trained to believe that life is all about facts. That, of course is a belief rather than a fact, and, as Dickens proceeds to show, it is a belief that ill-equips its disciples for life. His concern is not so much with a particular pedagogy as with the philosophy that is being perpetrated, which he is anxious to demonstrate as being both fallacious and dangerous.

As we consider the appropriate kind of education for Christian children, we should be aware that what is taught and the way that it is taught have far more significance than the simple content of what is being communicated. Teachers are not only pouring information into little heads; they are actually molding whole lives.

Jesus tells us that when students have completed their training, they will be like their teachers (Luke 6:40). He sees the crucial issue as being what kind of people they will be as a result of their education, not what kind of information they have accumulated. As parents consider where to send their child to school, this is the most fundamental factor. Who is the teacher? Do I want my child to end up being like him or her? It's not a matter of the information they will impart, nor their skill as a communicator, let alone the more peripheral matters like equipment and facilities upon which so many parents base their decision. It's a matter of being: he will "*be* like his teacher."

"Being" is a heart matter ("*As [a man] thinks in his heart, so is he*"— Proverbs 23:7). Touching children's hearts includes forming the presuppositions in their minds, stirring their emotions as to what they consider to be important, and motivating their will toward action. In one direction or another, all of these inevitably take place in any teaching context. This is the hidden curriculum that lies beneath the surface of the one presented in the text book or outlined in the school's publicity brochure. This is the course that sets the course for life. And as Jesus implies, it has more to do with the teacher than the material being taught.

We all know this to be true. How much do you remember of the pages of notes that you meticulously recorded during your school years? But have there not been a few key people who have impacted and changed the course of your life? We kid ourselves if we think education is about filling heads when, in reality, it is at least as much about touching hearts.

God has wired us that way. We say that the way to a man's heart is through his stomach, but the Bible tells us that the way to his heart is through his mind. Paul rejoiced that the Roman Christians *"...obeyed from the heart that form of doctrine to which [they] were delivered"* (Romans 6:17).

That is to say, the truth so gripped their mind that it moved their hearts. Ideas have consequences. God wired us that way.

Impacting Lives, not Imparting Information

Humanists have been smart enough to understand the connection between the head and the heart. Some of their leading thinkers consciously planned to use the educational process, in which it was assumed that students were being taught neutral, objective facts, to cause a heart-change in the lives of their young charges.

Christian Overman documents a meeting on September 12, 1905 in Peck's Restaurant in lower Manhattan. Five men gathered to discuss how to bring about a different social order in America.[4] Among those present were Upton Sinclair, Jack London, and Clarence Darrow. That day they founded the Intercollegiate Socialist Society, and their plans included the establishment of chapters of their new organization on college campuses throughout the nation.

In time, the organization's name was changed to the League for Industrial Democracy, with its specific purpose stated as "education for a new social order." John Dewey became the League's vice president in the 30's, by which time the League was operating in many colleges and universities. He became its president in 1941.

Five men in a restaurant can't change the world. But a plan hatched by such a small group, to take its ideas into the educational system, beginning at the university level and proceeding down from there, has truly had a profound effect, not merely on the thinking but also on the lives and actions of generations of young people. These were ideas that had consequences.

We may disagree with their philosophy, but we have to admire their strategy. We need, in the Christian education movement, men and women who see the bigger picture—parents and teachers who recognize that their task is to change a society by changing the hearts and minds of children. If that sounds like brainwashing, that's because it is! Our young people need to have their brains washed of all the erroneous ideas with which they have been filled. The Bible calls it the renewing of the mind (Romans 12:2), which is a renewal that takes place as we gradually become less and less conformed to the way that the world thinks.

We need to see what the Intercollegiate Socialist Society understood. The education system is all about training future generations how to think and preparing them to make a difference in their world. Ideas have consequences. We must use our classrooms to convey the ideas that are ultimately important, to present those ideas in a way that is consciously designed to achieve intended consequences.

This is why it is not enough for Christian schools and home-schoolers to simply take the standard public school text books and teach the same material, hoping that the safety of a Christian environment and the addition of some prayer and Bible verses will make the difference. The subject matter must be presented in the context of an explicit biblical worldview. This is not easy for teachers who learned all their material from the secular humanists.

Paul tells us that all things are to be for the glory of God—they are to be "*...of Him and through Him and to Him*" (Romans 11:36). If Paul says "all things," then *what* we teach and *how* we teach must fall into this category too! We must portray our academic information as it comes "from Him," relating our subject matter to the God who has created all things. It must be presented as being ultimately "to Him," reinforcing the need to use all that we learn to his glory. Such an educational outcome is only possible for believing teachers who, by God's grace, go about their duties "through Him," to complete the trinity of ideas in Romans 11:36. But sadly, when we teach out of the wisdom acquired in our secular training rather than "through Him," the teaching, even of Christian teachers, often shows little evidence that what we are talking about comes "of Him." And in that case, the end results of the time our students have spent with us will bear little fruit "for Him." Even Christian teachers, in Christian schools, when they are not teaching from an explicitly biblical worldview, can bear kinds of fruit that they would be saddened to see.

Many resources are now available to Christian parents and teachers. One particularly helpful resource comes from Christian Overman. In *Making the Connections*,[5] Overman has developed a practical means of ensuring that teachers learn how to integrate a biblical worldview into all their lesson plans. There will inevitably be consequences in the lives of our students as a result of what we teach and how we teach. We should plan for those consequences. We should consciously think though the relationship between the ideas and the intended consequences and deliberately plan to transform lives by the renewing of the mind.

Christian education is not about imparting information. It is about impacting lives. We want our students to grow up to be the world-changers that our culture so desperately needs. They don't have to become internationally famous. But they should change the personal worlds in which they will have influence as salt and light. This is the course laid out—the true curriculum of Christian education.

ENDNOTES

1. Charles Colson: How now shall we live, (Wheaton:Tyndale, 1999) p.332

2. Neil Postman & Charles Weingartner: Teaching as a subversive activity, (NY: Delta Books—Dell Publishing; 1969) p.84

3. Os Guiness: Fit bodies, fat minds, (Grand Rapids: Hourglass Books [Baker]; 1994) p.107

4. Christian Overman: Assumptions that affect our lives, (Chatsworth CA: Micah 6:8; 1996) p.234

5. Christian Overman & Don Johnson: Making the Connections (Biblical Worldview Institute; 2002—www.biblicalworldviewinstitute.org)

Chapter 6

Knowledge and Wisdom

Teachers sometimes think of themselves as being in the knowledge business. But Christian education, more accurately, concerns the wisdom business. This is not to say that knowledge is a purely cognitive exercise that can be separated from God; both wisdom and knowledge are alike in that both are properly rooted in the primacy of the fear of the Lord (Proverbs 1:7; 9:10). But wisdom certainly takes us beyond Gradgrind's world of facts, and it is in that broader territory that Christian education is to flourish. "Knowledge comes," wrote Tennyson, "but wisdom lingers." We might add that knowledge comes and goes, judging from the poor retention rate of much that is covered in the school curriculum. But wisdom is for life.

Wisdom Results in a Lifestyle

Wisdom has to do with the application of knowledge, what we do with what we know. We may make a comparison between pure science and technology, where the latter relates to the practical application of the abstract theories. Wisdom is applied knowledge, and that application is contingent upon character. What we do will depend on who we are.

Christian parents recognize that true wisdom begins with the fear of the Lord. As they consider the appropriate context in which their children are educated, they should bear in mind that this sort of fear is a biblically required part of God's curriculum for children. In Psalm 34:11, David tells us that the fear of the Lord can and should be taught to children. In essence, the fear of the Lord means a reverential, godly lifestyle.

The idea of "lifestyle" is important in the Bible, though the word is a modern one. In the vocabulary of the scriptures, the idea is often conveyed in the word "walk." The Greeks thought of knowledge as something to be understood in an intellectual sense, but for the Hebrews knowing the truth was meaningless apart from walking in the truth, to use a phrase that John employs (see 3 John chapter 3). To know the truth, whether about Jesus or about any other facet of life, we must walk in the truth. So, Paul exhorts us to walk worthy of the calling with which we were called (Ephesians 4:1). To use modern terminology, in our lifestyle we are to walk the talk. Talk can be a matter of knowledge, but walking implies wisdom.

The Bible teaches that there are various kinds of wisdom: some good, some bad, but wisdom nonetheless. Paul distinguishes between the wisdom of this age and the wisdom of God (1 Corinthians 2:6,7). This corresponds to the fact that there are different ways of walking—most "...*[walk] according to the course of this world*" (Ephesians 2:2), but we are to "*Walk as children of light*" (Ephesians 5:8). Of course, the way we walk depends on our view of reality; different kinds of walking result from different kinds of wisdom.

Whenever teaching happens, wisdom, values, and lifestyle are inevitably communicated. This may be a pagan or a godly wisdom, leading to pagan or godly ways of life, but wisdom as well as knowledge is always part of the package that comes when students sit at the feet of a teacher. As we have stressed, students become like their teacher (Luke 6:40). They learn from who teachers are as much as from what teachers say. If there is a conflict between what teachers say and who they are, students will always pick up on who they are. As Bob Mumford said, "You can say mumps as much as you like, but if you have measles, measles is what they will catch!" This fact makes it hard to comprehend how Christian parents can justify sending their children to be taught by non-Christian teachers.

Education may only Produce Educated Fools

Since wisdom cannot be divorced from character or behavior, but inevitably issues in a "walk," and since all education includes an impartation of wisdom as well as knowledge, we must conclude that education is a moral exercise. It has to do with behavior as much as the intellect. Truth is learned and understood as it is accepted and incarnated in the learner; it is perceived intellectually and then lived out.

Both knowledge and wisdom are predicated on the fear of the Lord in biblical thought, so a Hebrew model of education was necessarily built on a moral foundation. Knowledge apart from virtue was considered vanity. Even worse than that, to add knowledge to those without virtue seems unwise in that, as has been said, "The world already has enough educated fools."

Many western students see their education as little more than an accumulation of information, and the development of certain mental and physical skills. How far removed this is from a biblical model! As Marvin Wilson points out in *The Jewish Concept of Learning—a Christian Appreciation:*

> In the Greek world, teaching primarily involved the transference of knowledge in the intellectual and technical areas, e.g. music, art, riding, reading or fencing. Thus a teacher taught his pupil certain rules or procedures which hopefully would develop any aptitude that pupil might possess. If his reasoning powers needed development, then intellectual exercises were provided; if his body needed training, then sports and physical exercise were stressed; if greater manual dexterity was needed, then art or sculpture might be taught. In short, in secular Greek literature, the *didaskolos* (teacher) aimed mainly at developing the talents and potentialities of his pupil. Unlike the idea of teaching in the Jewish world, his teaching did not usually concern itself with the development of the student's whole personality, and his education in the deepest sense.[1]

This approach to education was an inevitable consequence of the philosophical atmosphere of the Greek world—an atmosphere saturated with dualism. The philosophy of men like Socrates and Plato envisioned an entirely separate world of ideals, metaphysical concepts far above the lower level of temporal physical matter. The dichotomy extended to man himself, as Plato downgraded the body and exalted the soul, calling the body the "prison house of the soul." Artists and philosophers were honored in that culture, while manual laborers were degraded. This remains a danger that is perpetuated in much of our modern educational system with its focus on academic grades, which tend to be the benchmark for a student's sense of self worth. We must recognize how unbiblical this dichotomy within the human personality really is.

Educating Whole People

Certainly the Bible refers to different aspects of man's being (body, soul, spirit). But there is no sense of higher and lower, and certainly no chasm between what we think in our heads and what we do in our bodies. The Greek model assumes that the head can be effectively severed from the real person and then fed and filled in isolation from the rest of life.

In evangelical jargon, we have tended to perpetuate the same dichotomy. We talk of the longest drop as being the few inches from the head to the heart, bemoaning our slowness to become excited about that which we understand in a theoretical way. The desire to integrate the responses of the head and the heart in this way is an important step toward reducing this dualism, but it still plays into the hands of the false dichotomy by its portrayal of these distinct anatomical parts!

The Bible is much more consistent in its references to human beings in a holistic sense. In Hebrew thought there was little distinction between head and heart because the very notion of heart in Scripture includes mind, will, and emotions. Perhaps within that unified sense of being, the head might represent the realm of thoughts, and, if there had to be an anatomical distinction, the emotions were seen as seated in the bowels (usually translated more delicately as "innermost being). But the heart is the integrating reality of who we are.

As we have pointed out, the Bible speaks of us as thinking in our hearts (Proverbs 23:7), a strange idea to modern ears. But, taking this together with our observation that both wisdom and knowledge are to start in the fear of the Lord, it is significant to hear the cry of the psalmist that God would "...*unite [his] heart to fear [God's] name!*" (Psalm 86:11). This is a prayer that there would be no dichotomy, that the whole being would be united in its reverence for the Lord, issuing in a godly lifestyle as all that one knows (thoughts), all that one feels about what he knows (emotions), and all that one chooses to do with what he knows (will) will be integrated in walking in the ways of the Lord.

This is the mandate of Christian education. We are heart surgeons more than brainwashers. The teacher's task is not complete until he or she has not only provided information, but also aroused passion about that subject matter: passions of *worship*, as the knowledge is seen to be revelatory of the nature of God, and passions of *enthusiasm* to see that information worked out in life in ways that will bring glory to God. But this is not merely an emotional passion, though teachers and students should be genuinely excited about what they are studying. It is a passion that engages the will and results in a godly lifestyle in which all that has been learned is put to good use for the benefit of mankind and the glory of God.

Learning and Being

Learning relates to being, not just knowing. From what we have said about the importance of viewing the student as a whole person, not merely a disconnected head waiting to be filled with information, it will be clear by now that there must be a greater focus on who we are than what we know.

North American culture emerged from Puritan roots. The Puritans have been much maligned in recent years, but if we are looking for historic examples of the biblical model of education being fruitfully worked out in practice, there are few clearer illustrations.

John Milton, the famous Puritan leader in seventeenth century England, articulated their philosophy of education. It was mentioned earlier that he thought of education as restoration. We will now consider the next idea he put forward. In *On Education*, he wrote, "The end then of learning is to repair the ruins of our first parents by regaining to know God aright, and out of that knowledge to love him, to imitate him, to be like him, as we may the nearest by possessing our souls of true virtue." As Christian Overman[2] points out, Milton did not see education as primarily a matter of developing the brains, talents, and potential of the individual, but rather as the development of a whole person. Education's goal is to be like God—a matter of *being* rather than *knowing* or *doing*.

When we, with our modern mindsets, read such words, we fear that school is somehow being transformed into Sunday school, or that the goal of a Christian high school is to become a kind of junior level Bible school, institutions devoted to introspective, mystical, religious detachment from life. But that impression only serves to further emphasize the dualism that has taken hold of our thinking, for to us, such "spiritual" pursuits are dichotomized from normal living. There was no such separation in Milton's thinking. His reasons for becoming "like God" were very practical and down to earth. In the same treatise he went on to say, "I call therefore a complete and generous education that which fits a man to perform justly, and skillfully, and magnanimously, all the offices, both private and public, of peace and war."

This was the Puritan view of life and of education. They were compelled by a vision of seeing practical Christianity at work in competent expressions in all of life, including both public and private affairs. They were not interested only in building a pure church, but a whole culture. That was why they had come to the New World with a vision of creating a "city set on a hill," as one of their leaders, John Winthrop, had put it. They sought to prepare not only godly pastors and parents, but also godly civil servants and skilled citizens. Each person was to be a productive member of society and a faithful citizen living harmoniously under God in a justly governed society. That vision required a caliber of *being* in its citizens, as well as competence in *doing* and proficiency in *knowing*.

The emphasis on godly character or virtue was never conceived as being a religious appendage to the rest of life. Theirs was a worldview that saw all of life as sacred and everything under the dominion of God. No sacred/secular divide existed there, and no one thought of limiting themselves to only so-called "religious" concerns. Seeing all of creation as God's creation, they saw value in the pursuit of all spheres of knowledge and study, though keeping all subject to the final authority of Scripture. They valued not only book learning, but manual labor too. As one of their number put it, a Christian can regard "his shop as well as his chapel as holy ground" (George Swinnock in *The Christian Man's Calling*). They understood the implications of the fact that the activities of craftsmen and artisans making furniture and garments for the Mosaic tabernacle were performed by people "endowed with the Spirit of wisdom" (Exodus 28:3); they were every bit as much anointed as the priests and prophets.

The Puritans serve as a model to us, reminding us that we too need godly lawyers, politicians, doctors, educators, carpenters, mechanics, and used car salesmen who see their work as being *"...as to the Lord"* (Colossians 3:23). Every endeavor is to be competently carried out as part of the Dominion Mandate of ruling the earth as God's vice-regents to His glory. A biblical education must seek to see students "endowed with a Spirit of wisdom," wisdom that is not simply the wisdom of knowing countless Bible verses, but the wisdom that enables them to be first-class craftsmen and artisans. We need to be producing those lawyers, politicians, carpenters—and every other profession and trade—if we are to see God's kingdom come, God's will being done on earth as it is in heaven, and that city that is from above being set on a hill here on earth as Winthrop dreamed. But note the adjective that begins the list that we have constructed at the start of the paragraph: they are to be *godly* lawyers, politicians, and judges."

The kinds of students we should yearn to see graduating from our Christian schools and home-schooling programs are young people like Daniel. He is described as showing *"...intelligence in every branch of wisdom, endowed with understanding, and discerning knowledge"* (Daniel 1:4).

That is why he could serve the kings of his day with such fruitfulness. But those talents and intellectual accomplishments were only effective in serving the purposes of God's kingdom, as opposed to merely advancing Daniel's own career, because of who Daniel was as a man. It was his character, his moral fortitude, and his godliness that enabled him to be effective to God's glory.

The Puritans understood this. As a result of their legacy, the concern of early American Christians for education was that it be a means to honor God in all of life. Yale University, for example, was established in 1701 to be an institution where "youth may be instructed in the Arts and Sciences who through the blessing of God Almighty may be fitted for Public employment both in Church and Civil State." But unless we focus on the spiritual and moral dimensions of our students' lives, unless we wrestle with the issues of who they are as well as what they know and what they are equipped to do, the irony is that even Christian schools may produce competent graduates who go on to further the cause of the kingdom of darkness!

This is no empty concern. Karl Marx went to a Christian school. At least, when his Jewish father became a Protestant following a Prussian decree in 1816 that banned Jews from the higher ranks of law and medicine, he had his children baptized and enrolled his son, Karl, in what had been a Jesuit high school. By that time, however, it was liberal and secularized. Paul Johnson writes, "Marx was confirmed at fifteen and for a time seems to have been a passionate Christian."[3] Some of his school-boy essays reveal his sensitive studies in the Gospels. How ironic that the graduate of a Jesuit high school should later write of religion as "the opium of the people. The abolition of religion, as the illusory happiness of men, is a demand for their real happiness." How sad that his learning and skills should be put to such devastating use in the fight *against* Christianity.

Learning and Doing

We have seen that learning relates to being, not just to knowing. But it also relates to doing. A Christian curriculum must have a practical outcome: it is a course that lays out a race to be run. Certainly biblical education aims to produce *godly* citizens. It must be concerned about the character qualities of the people who graduate to fill these roles. But Christian education does not stop at the word *godly*. Having focused on the students' being, it must move on to their doing. A knowledge-based education is insufficient, and so is a character-based education. These two vital foundations must take us to the consideration of what students, given who they are, will do with what they know. As in the Puritan model, they must be equipped to take their place as productive members of society, whether in politics, business, or whatever sphere of honest work.

The Greeks, from whom much of the thinking of the modern Western world is derived, were largely content to learn in order to simply comprehend. The knowing was a sufficient end in itself. The Hebrews, on the other hand, learned in order to do. Even the Rabbis, the religious teachers, were expected to know a trade. For example, the famous Rabbi Hillel was a woodcutter, the apostle Paul was a tentmaker, and even Jesus was a carpenter. No academic ivory tower for them. They were not ashamed of physical labor. In fact, the Jewish Talmud explicitly repudiates any possibility of dualism when it says, "Just as a man is required to teach his Son Torah [the Law], so is he required to teach him a trade" (Kiddushin 29a).

Learning for Doing

Too many students find school confusing because they cannot see a connection between what they are learning and the life that they expect to lead. If what they are studying is a course, it is a course that does not seem to lead anywhere. As a result, they are unmotivated, feeling that what they are studying is pointless. In terms of real life, it often is.

The most common form of reward in the traditional educational system has to do with the awarding of grades. Why do students learn? Most learn in order to pass exams. That goal completed, they are happy to forget all that they learned. In the earlier years of school, the passing of exams has little to do with moving on to a higher form of education, or to being able to get a good job. It has more to do with getting a good report card and all the affirmation that comes from a parent who glows over the long list of high marks. That affirmation is all that is needed for some students to endure a term of study.

But perhaps the aspiration to achieve high grades is not an appropriate form of primary motivation. Many children quickly figure out that it is an impossible dream, no matter how hard they try. On average, only 10% of the class will get straight "A's," and the other 90% is smart enough to recognize which members of the class have a realistic chance of competing for those few available places and to know that they are not one of them. For the majority of students, the prospect of above average grades is an impossibility, if for no other reason than the obvious statistical fact that if the affirmation goes to the "above average," most have to be average or below!

It is unreasonable to motivate simply by offering the carrot of successful grade averages. Instead, we should encourage children to learn in order to be able to do, not simply in order to be able to pass exams. Some educational theories emphasize the merits of learning *by* doing (Dewey spoke of learning by doing; Postman writes, "It's not what you say to people that counts; it is what you have them do"[4]). There is certainly much to be said for that: in a practical apprenticeship program, learning takes place in a hands-on environment rather than in the abstraction of the classroom. Some children will be motivated in such a practical context, but that is not quite what we are saying. Jay Adams places the emphasis rather differently when he suggest that the biblical model is not so much learning *by* doing as it is learning *for* doing.[5]

Even when the truth being communicated is theological truth, the biblical focus is on truth for use. Truth is never taught for its own sake, but always for practical application. So, for example, Paul wrote to Titus about God's people coming to "*...the acknowledgment of the truth **which accords with godliness**"* (Titus 1:1, emphasis added).

To know the truth to the point where we can reproduce the facts in a test is inadequate. That kind of academic excellence is not truly excellent. Our goal must be that our students know the truth to the point where they can put it into practice. Their learning must be oriented toward doing.

"Teaching...to Observe"

We see this clearly in Jesus' discipleship model. In His final instruction to His students as to how they were to go about their task of making more students, Jesus stated that their aim was to be "*...teaching them to observe all things that I have commanded you"* (Matthew 28:20).

Note the goal of His educational methodology: teaching...to observe. Of course, when He says "observe" here, He is not expecting the students to be onlookers; He means that they are to be considered proficient students when they have reached the point where they are putting into practice in daily living what they have learned in the classroom.

What greater motivation can there be for our students than seeing that all that they are learning is not merely important because the grades on their next report card depend on it, but rather because all they are learning is deliberately and effectively equipping them for life and ministry! They may be learning about pigs in an elementary science class, but actually they are learning how to be more effective practitioners of the Dominion Mandate, which calls us to rule over all the God has created as His vice-regents to his glory. In the terminology of Genesis 2, they are learning to "name the animals" so as to be able to rule. They are learning for doing. And they have been properly taught when they have learned how to integrate what they have been taught into daily living, not when they score 80% on a quiz.

In order for teachers to be effective in this model of education, they need to be able to demonstrate the importance of *using* what they teach, enabling students to see the feasibility of applying what they are learning. Teachers must instruct young people in how they can use what is taught. This will require a teaching strategy that includes the use of practical projects—not necessarily the projects where students reproduce the facts they have learned on a nicely colored piece of poster-board, but projects where they have to put what they have learned into practice in the real world. They need to see that what they have learned makes a difference. It will also require a teaching strategy that places an emphasis on problem solving, with the problems being as realistic as possible within the limitations of their theoretical knowledge at that point in the student's academic career.

Does this mean there is no place for the abstraction of pure mathematics, or that the finer points of grammar are unimportant? Not at all! But it does mean that these important areas must be learned in the context of persuading the students that there are significant practical implications for learning what, in their naivety, they think is irrelevant. We must demonstrate that it is relevant, and this is best done by teachers who themselves are passionate about the excitement of what they see being done (or better still, what they themselves are doing) with the subject matter they have mastered.

There is no classroom scene in the Bible. To the contrary, the Bible says that the best place for children to learn is in real life. They are to be taught, as Deuteronomy 6:7-9 explains, "...*when you sit in your house, when you walk by the way, when you lie down, and when you rise up.*" Instructions are to be posted not on chalkboards, but "on the doorposts of your house and on your gates." In fact, Post-It notes might make the ideas stick when you look at them in the context of what you are doing with your hands! Does that mean we should do away with classrooms? Not necessarily. But our classrooms must become places where, even in an apparently artificial environment, we recreate contexts which approximate to real life so that students can learn *by* observing (seeing) and *for* observing (doing). This is what will make the classrooms come alive, far more alive than lots of brightly colored posters on the wall.

The visual impact that our students need is not the visual impact of pictures; it is the visual impact of seeing truth at work.

Some students who will never study mathematics for tests will study technological intricacies (even mathematical ones) when that research is connected with motorbikes they want to maintain. For the academically inclined, it is sufficient motivation for them to study if they see the affirmation that they will gain in a good test score. But for most students, the necessary motivation is more likely to be in a motorbike or its equivalent on their list of interests and passions. They will learn for doing. For our part we must ensure that all that we want them to learn is going to be useful.

Doing for Serving

Learning for doing could apply to any form of education. But we are concerned primarily with Christian education, so we must take this desire to learn for doing to the next stage. Christian young people learn in order to do, in order to serve. The life skills they learn must not only be seen as useful for the students themselves, but useful in enabling them to serve God and other people. They must learn not merely to do, but also to give. That which they do with their education in real life will be part of their calling to glorify God.

Thus, to use an example that Adams gives[6], they learn grammar in order to be able to write effectively. They learn to do, but what they do takes the form of service. They put their newly acquired writing skills into practice in expressions of ministry. For instance, older students learn to write stories for younger pupils, or they learn to write plays and skits that can be performed in open-air evangelism, or they learn to write letters to the editor which they will have the joy of seeing published. Their goal is not to pass tests or to get good grades on a report card. Their goal is to see that what they do can be pleasing to God. Effective writing opens up opportunities; for a Christian, those opportunities are opportunities to serve.

Our goal is not simply to enable students to pass our tests. It is to equip young people to be and to do all that God has for them. Certainly they need a lot of information to arrive at that destination. But our task is not done when their heads are full of facts. It is done when they have been taught to observe all that the Lord has commanded.

The fruit of Christian education will not be seen in the marks and grades that they score in comparison with their peers in a public school, though there is no excuse for Christians settling for a lower academic standard. The real fruit will be seen in who our alumni are and in what they are doing in the years that follow their time under our care. We dare not minimize the significance of the formative role we are inevitably having. As Winston Churchill once said, "Headmasters have power at their disposal with which Prime Ministers have never been invested." May that power be used to raise a generation who will serve the Lord with all their strength!

ENDNOTES

1. Quoted by Overman: Assumptions that affect our lives (Chatsworth CA: Micah 6:8; 1996) p.225f

2. ibid, p.239

3. Paul Johnson: Intellectuals, (London: Weidenfield and Nicolson; 1988) p.53

4. Neil Postman & Charles Weingartner: Teaching as a subversive activity, (NY: Delta Books—Dell Publishing; 1969) p.19

5. Jay Admas: Back to the Blackboard, (Phillipsburg: ; 1982) p.90

6. ibid, p.126

Part 4

The Assumptions of our Curriculum:

Christian Education Adopts Hebrew rather than
Greek Thinking Patterns

Chapter 7

The Cultural Divide between Hebrews and Greeks

We began our consideration of curriculum with an illustration about a fighter pilot who crashed because she was disoriented. Her assumption that she was the right way up resulted in a fiery conflagration. When she thought she was maneuvering into a steep ascent, she dove rapidly into the ground. A wrong assumption led to a fatal error.

Assumptions are important. As the title of philosopher Richard Weaver's book puts it, "Ideas have consequences." But the dilemma with assumptions that drastically affect our thinking and our actions is that, by their very nature, they largely go unquestioned. Although we are often unaware of our own worldview, it determines the outcome of our actions. Evangelical Christians generally agree that God's revelation in Scripture is the basis for our thinking, but we may not appreciate how much we view that revelation through the lens of a worldview that has been formed to some degree by other ideas and assumptions. Our interpretation of Scripture may reveal as much about our assumptions as it does about the text itself.

Few of us make the effort to question our assumptions. We naively assume that our thinking is rooted in a Judeo-Christian mindset. As "Westerners," we believe that to some degree our Western civilization reflects biblical assumptions.

A Clash of Worldviews

We recognize that our way of thinking is very different than thinking in other parts of the world. We would agree with Charles Colson's statement that, "The world is divided not so much by geographic boundaries as by religious and cultural traditions, by people's most deeply held beliefs—by worldviews."[1] Colson explains that this led to Harvard scholar Samuel Huntington's celebrated prediction of a coming clash between the worldviews of the three major traditional civilizations: the Western world, the Islamic world, and the Confucian East. The current "War on Terrorism" initially appears to fit this interpretation. But Colson sides with an alternative view proposed by one of Huntington's former students, political scientist James Kurth. Kurth contends that the most significant clash will be *within* Western civilization itself—between those who adhere to a Judeo-Christian framework and those who favor post-modernism and multi-culturalism.

This clash of worldviews is ultimately a clash of assumptions. It is a conflict between groups of people who think differently. Christian education should challenge us to think about our thinking, about the way we think about the facts. Creationists and Evolutionists have the same facts before them, yet they come to entirely different conclusions, with both claiming to do justice to the facts. So how do we think?

We can no longer assume that we in the West are thinking in biblical ways. Perhaps we should never have assumed that we were. The skeptical rejection of moral absolutes in postmodernism is starkly unbiblical, but the modernism which preceded it was no more biblical, with its pragmatic pursuit of technological progress and material success and its elevation of individualism. These are but some of the characteristics of the worldview that has shaped modern evangelicalism. It is a sobering thought that, while we would like to think that our culture has been shaped by the gospel, it may be more realistic to recognize that evangelicalism has been significantly affected by the mindset of the world from which it has emerged.

Some would argue that Western civilization has been departing from its Judeo-Christian presuppositions since the day in 1610 when Rene Descartes concluded, "I think, therefore I am." In this simple postulate he summarized an idea that has been a fundamental assumption in centuries of Western thinking—that man is the fixed point around which all revolves and that human reason is the foundation upon which all is to be understood.

Descartes did not reach his conclusion in a vacuum. Centuries earlier, Greek philosophers had built their culture on the assumption that human reason was a sufficient starting point for determining truth, for measuring values, and for molding morality. The idea that "man is the measure of all things" goes back to that era. For those of us who live in what is known as the Western world, our cultural roots go back to two historic starting points: the ancient Greeks and the ancient Hebrews. Descartes represents one side of a deep-rooted intellectual tradition that continues to draw on the ancient Greek heritage. His ideas served to promote substantial doubts concerning the God-centeredness and the moral certainties of the other ancient tradition, the Hebrew worldview.

Perhaps it is in this light that we see the basis of Kurth's prediction of a coming clash within Western civilization, a clash of even more far-reaching significance than the clash between Western and Islamic cultures. It is a clash that reflects the inherent instability of Western culture. Our culture has been built upon a massive intellectual fault line that lies beneath everything that has been built. The cultural earthquake will be the result of the shift between the two plates of Greek and Hebrew assumptions. The outcome reflects Jesus' warning that anything built on a foundation other than obedience to His Word is existing on borrowed time; its eventual collapse is inevitable. The wind and the rain of which Jesus spoke may represent a philosophical storm as much as a meteorological one.

If we pursue the analogy of geological plates and a dividing fault line, it is probably true to say that most evangelicals stand with one foot on each plate, and much of the modern church is built straddling the same divide. This is becoming an increasingly uncomfortable posture as the two worldviews drift further apart! But as we consider the implications of this for education, our goal is to ensure that all that we build is securely built on the only foundation that lasts. The Bible frequently stresses the danger of "mixture," and nowhere is this more important than in the realm of foundations.

That is why it is vital to consider the contrast between the two great cultural traditions of the Greeks and Hebrews, noting Paul's awareness of the significance of this contrast for the progress of the gospel. We shall see how much of what we do in the realm of education is built on a shaky foundation. We need to enter into the dark crawlspace underneath the structure of Christian education and examine the assumptions upon which all is built. In this journey, we shall largely follow the path led by Christian Overman in his important book, *Assumptions that Affect our Lives*.[2] He writes about this great cultural divide as an educator.

Paul's Concerns about Greeks and Hebrews

Paul was aware of the fundamentally different worldviews of the Jews and the Greeks. Both were antagonistic to the gospel, but for different reasons. He summed this up in his statement that the Jews were looking for miraculous signs and the Greeks were seeking wisdom (1 Corinthians 1:22). These perspectives, as Gordon Fee points out, "illustrate the basic idolatries of humanity. God must function as the all-powerful or the all-wise, but always in terms of our best interests—power in our behalf and wisdom like ours! For the ultimate idolatry is that of insisting that God conform to our own prior views [assumptions] as to how 'the God who makes sense' ought to do things."[3]

In the context of 1 Corinthians, while Paul takes issue with the false expectations of many Jews of his day, his real target is the fascination with wisdom that preoccupied many in the Corinthian church. He wanted to address the Greek assumptions that still dominated their thinking despite the fact that they had now become Christians.

The Jews had their problems. Many of them had demanded signs of Jesus. Jews demanded that the God who had acted powerfully on their behalf in history would do so again in the form of a Messiah who conformed to their political aspirations. But in 1 Corinthians, Paul is not primarily taking issue with the worldview of his forefathers. When, in another context, he is contrasting Jewish and Gentile thinking, he is clear that the Jews had the profound advantage of being those to whom were committed to the oracles of God (Romans 3:2). Paul's concern at this point is with the distortion of that thinking that demanded the power of God be made to function within the limitations of their false expectations and in the cause of their self-interests. Paul continues to think as a Jew, as one whose culture has been molded by the privilege of being the recipient of the Word of God. However, he thinks as a Jew whose thinking has been freed from the distortions of the Judaism of his day.

In Corinthians, Paul's target is Greek thought patterns. He clearly understands that God is all-wise as well as all-powerful. He recognized that the Greek pursuit of wisdom was a national characteristic, noted as early as Herodotus who said, "All Greeks were zealous for every kind of learning." Who can fault them for that? As a result they had pioneered great advances in civilization. But their idolatry was to conceive of God as Ultimate Reason, meaning of course what we deem to be reasonable. But, as Paul goes on to demonstrate, in the apparent foolishness of the Cross, God's "folly" turns out to be far wiser than human wisdom (1 Corinthians 1:25). As Fee puts it, "In the Cross, God 'outsmarted' his human creatures and thereby nullified their wisdom."[4] With this point established, Paul proceeds to challenge the Greek philosophical assumptions still affecting the minds and behavior of the Corinthian believers. These assumptions are in many ways at the root of most of the problems he addresses in that church. He pleads for a wisdom that is "not of this age" (1 Corinthians 2:6), a completely different way of thinking about life.

To those of us who consider ourselves to be part of Western civilization, this warning must be taken seriously. Those who are deemed to be "wise" in terms of the thinking of the age must actually go through the process of becoming foolish in order to be re-programmed in true wisdom (1 Corinthians 3:18). Those of us who consider ourselves to be educated have much to un-learn.

Most people who are involved in education have learned to think within the educational system that they are perpetuating. Christian teachers may have been taught doctrine by pastors, but they have been taught education by humanists. Paul is asking us to step back and consider how much of our thinking is actually an expression of the wisdom of this age, which God characterizes as foolishness. To continue to trust in the way of thinking which has characterized our culture, Paul says, is a delusion. We are called to challenge the assumptions in our thinking, and insofar as our worldview has been affected by the philosophies of the world, we are to recognize those philosophies as foolish and futile (1 Corinthians 3:19).

But the Greek philosophies that Paul was so concerned about have not been buried and lost in antiquity. They are, in part at least, the very roots of our Western culture, and thereby, the source of much of our thinking today. So how much of this Greek thinking, with which Paul takes issue in Corinthians and elsewhere, has permeated our view of education? We should honestly examine how much the way we think differs fundamentally from a biblical mindset. Parents contemplating an education for their children in a Christian school or in a home-schooling program must assess their options in light of the comparison between the wisdom of the world and the ways of the Lord.

Some Practical Differences between Greek and Hebrew Thought

We mentioned in Chapter 2 the scene in which a bridegroom turns to his young bride and whispers in her ear, "My darling, your belly is like a heap of wheat!" In our culture, the likely outcome is a major row, but when Solomon spoke these very words to a young lady 3,000 years ago (in Song of Solomon 7:2), she went weak at the knees with delight at the compliment. What assumptions lie behind the very different responses to these words?

In a Hebrew mindset, the primary concern is on essence rather than form or image. The words did not necessarily denote a big round stomach (if that is what came to mind when you read Solomon's words, you are thinking like a Greek!). The beauty of his young bride was not primarily seen in terms of shape; Solomon's description had nothing to do with what he saw with his eyes but with what she evoked in his soul. The essence of a heap of wheat is a bountiful harvest. Solomon is not saying that his young bride *looks like* a heap of wheat, but that he sees her as being abundantly fruitful in many areas of life.

Similarly, in the references that he goes on to make about her large nose and long neck, he is not intending that we draw a portrait based on his description. We are supposed to understand the kind of person she was. In that regard, these symbols of strength are more important to the bridegroom than our Western preoccupation with the kind of physical beauty that is splashed across the pages of our fashion magazines. In like manner, we note the total absence of any details about Jesus' physical appearance in the Gospels: it was a Greek culture that insisted on visual representations in pictures and statues. The Gospels were content to tell us what kind of man He was. How different are these two ways of thinking! Yet our visual culture of magazines and movies leaves no doubt as to whether we are thinking more like Greeks than Hebrews.

Consider the description in the Bible of Noah's Ark. We are given details of the construction of a big, sea-worthy vessel, but we have no idea of whether it had a pointed, rounded, or square bow. Functionality was what mattered; external form came second. The Greeks, on the other hand, were so concerned with appearance that, for example, as they pioneered classical wonders of architectural design, they sometimes built their columns wider at the top, tapering down toward the base to distort the perspective of distance and make the appearance more appealing to the senses.

Perhaps in even these apparently trivial references to the importance of "appearances" we can see something of the way that our thinking has been culturally molded. Remember: all of us are disciples of somebody! We prefer to think of ourselves as being "our own person," as if we had made up our own mind about issues. But, as Willard points out, that is only because we have been discipled by those who taught us that this is what we should be and do.[5] Ironically, we came to the conclusion that we are to be individualists through dependence on the ideas of others! We came to believe that we can trust our own reason because the reasoning of others pointed us in that direction. Our minds have been molded and always bear the fingerprints of a life of discipleship. We have been discipled by the culture at whose feet we have sat in classrooms and movie theatres, in books and in music. To become a disciple of Jesus is to learn to start thinking differently. It starts with a call to repent, which could be understood as a call "to think about how we have been thinking."[6]

But let us consider some of the other assumptions that dominated the mindset of ancient Greece. Overman[7] draws up a list of characteristics of ancient Greece recorded by historian Will Durant in his famous book, *The Life of Greece*. Notice in the list that all of these things are commonplace in modern society and yet strangely unfamiliar in the Hebrew culture of the Jews in the Bible:

* People, especially the educated, rejected traditional religion;

* Men practiced manners that had previously been considered effeminate;

* The upper class was consumed with the pursuit of pleasure;

* Education stressed knowledge more than character and produced masses of half-educated people;

* Public games turned into professional contests;

* Homosexuality was popular;

* Men had easy access to watching dances by unclad women;

* The dramas of the day were full of seduction and adultery;

* A women's liberation movement brought women into active roles in a culture that had previously been male dominated;

* Motherhood was devalued and the bearing of children was considered an inconvenience; and

* Abortion was commonly practiced.

Durant describes these characteristics toward the end of his book in a subsection entitled "The Morals of Decay." This was Greece near the end of her life. But while ancient Greece came to an end, her ideas have lived on. Overman's argument is that it is the still-living Greek assumptions that continue to lead to inevitable moral decline. They have infiltrated our culture, increasingly displacing Judeo-Christian values. Because they are assumptions, they continue to undermine in a largely un-noticed way. What are some of those assumptions? In the next chapter we shall highlight some ways in which these assumptions have significantly influenced our thinking about education.

ENDNOTES

1. Charles Colson: How now shall we live (Wheaton: 999) p.19

2. Christian Overman: Assumptions that affect our lives (Chatsworth CA: Micah 6:8 ; 1996)

3. Gordon Fee: The First Epistle to the Corinthians (Grand Rapids: NICNT—Eerdmans; 1987) p.74

4. ibid p.77

5. Dallas Willard: The Divine Conspiracy (HarperSanFransisco; 1998) p.271

6. ibid p.325

7. op cit, p.30

Chapter 8

Greek Assumptions that have affected Education

Ideas have consequences, but ideas also have roots. We are exploring the fact that much of our thinking comes from the roots of the Ancient Greeks, but some of these Greek ideas appear very modern when they re-emerge in today's educational thinking. The traditional school curriculum abounds with examples.

Assumptions about Science

Who gives us snow: God or Mother Nature? The Jews clearly understood God to be the Creator of all things. But even Christians who are very cautious about what their children watch on television often let them watch "harmless" wildlife programs. They are considered harmless because of their lack of sex or violence, but perhaps they are equally dangerous in other ways. There, the young viewers will be taught about Mother Nature as the source of all things. Nature is always referred to with a capital "N." Such programs are a veritable worship service, as the viewing millions sit in awe, contemplating the wonders of what Nature has done. Nature seems to function by its own self-created laws, and we hear constantly of its power and its creativity. The questions about the origins of life become simple to answer: Life made itself; it's a product of Nature.

Darwinianism is not a modern notion. A Greek called Thales, sometimes referred to as "the Father of Western Philosophy," is credited with what historians have called the Ionian Science of Nature. He was the man who broke the spell of older views of numerous gods around Mount Olympus determining the outcome of natural events. In recent times, philosophers started saying, "God is dead!" But back in ancient Greece, secular thought was born with the Ionian's "gods are dead" movement, as Thales insisted that all that existed was nature. His follower, Anaximander, took this to the next step when he ventured an explanation for the origins of life. He proposed a theory that the first living things developed in water. Man, said Anaximander, "sprang from a different animal, in fact from a fish, which at first he resembled."[1]

All this pre-dates Darwin by some 2500 years. The idea that man previously existed in the form of "a different animal" goes back to the Greeks. Darwin was not an original thinker. The most famous of all Greek scientists, Aristotle, believed that the ape was an intermediate form of man. Aristotle classified man as an animal and then distinguished him from other animals in just one significant way. Man is unique in that he is a rational animal—an animal, but a rational one.

An assumption had been planted in the thinking of a culture. The assumption was and is that Mother Earth had given birth to every type of plant and animal, and Nature, with its relentless stream of energy pulling all towards its supra-rational fate, was the life-force which, as Obi-wan Kenobi said in *Star Wars* "binds the galaxy together." Resurrected by the ideas of Charles Darwin, the "Force" is now a religious assumption, displacing the Lord Jesus Christ whom the Scriptures declare holds all things together by His powerful word.

The Hebrews, on the other hand, worshipped a God who was both all-powerful (which none of the old Greek gods ever were in their constant feuds with one another) and entirely personal. The Greeks, before their secular revolution, had thought of their gods as very man-like; in fact it was the limitations of their human-likeness that prompted more sophisticated Greek philosophers to reject them. But the Hebrews followed the revelation of the Scriptures and therefore were not bound by the limitations of their finite reason. Consequently, without any sense of contradiction, they worshipped a God who was, both an infinitely powerful Creator with none of the limitations of humanity, and at the same time, infinitely personal. He was powerful enough to call the universe into being with a word and personal enough to visit with Abraham for a barbeque under the shade of a tree. In ultimate power and in personal intervention, He is perpetually involved in every detail of the wind and the rain, responding to prayer to dry up the rain, suspending the scientific "laws" at will.

We dare not assume that God is only present in the moments of miracle. As Overman says, "He is equally active and present in raising someone from the dead or in raising bread at 4.00 a.m. in the local bakery."[2] Our assumptions about God and reality affect science far more than at the point of discussing origins. As Christians we tend to imagine that if we have resisted the spirit of the age in regard to evolution, we can then do science with everybody else, as if somehow we are dealing with "brute facts," facts untempered by ideas. But there are vastly divergent views of science. Our worldview affects all that we do. Science that is built solely on human reason is only capable of building houses that will inevitably collapse beneath the winds that the Creator insists on blowing within His creation which, He refuses to vacate.

Assumptions about Man

Clearly the Hebrew presupposition was that man is made in the image of God. On the other hand, according to Thales and his followers, our "father" was water. But unless the assumption about man being made in the image of God is maintained, there is no true source of value or worth in human beings. The implications of this were all too obvious in ancient Greece.

The Spartans only considered their babies worthy of life if they satisfied the criteria of physical strength and health that were considered the paramount virtues in that culture. Weak or undersized babies were removed from their parents' care by officials determined to maintain the highest standards of strength in the society. They were then hurled over the cliffs of Mt. Taygetus. The "survival of the fittest" is not a new idea.

The survivors were taken from their parents at seven years of age and handed over to the military training program that was to be their home in a culture of statist collectivism. The only value in human life was seen in the strength and bravery that the individual might be able to contribute for the good of the State.

A few hundred miles away in Athens, we find a contrasting ideology: here it was the individual whose rights were exalted and upheld. In art, athletics, and education, and in the pursuit of personal pleasure, values were established in terms of self-expression. But infanticide was just as common as in Sparta. It was promoted on the basis of the "good life." Infants who might spoil their parents' quality of life were quickly disposed of, usually by exposure. Infanticide was also promoted as a safeguard against overpopulation and depletion of natural resources that might threaten the quality of life of the survivors. Those children who did survive were then thoroughly spoiled, indulged with all kinds of pleasures and free to pursue all kinds of self-expression.

Not surprisingly, when war erupted between Sparta and Athens, the soft-skinned Athenians were no match for the hardened Spartan warriors. In one sense it was a war between two ideologies. But while the two city-states differed in the way they determined human worth (collectivism vs. individualism), they shared the same bottom-line assumption. That assumption was best summarized by one of their own, Protagoras, who declared, "Man is the measure of all things." Whether man was perceived as individual man or collective man, it all stopped there.

Rabbi Daniel Lapin has written a telling book called *America's Real War*, in which he describes, from the viewpoint of an orthodox Jew, the contrast between the Judeo-Christian worldview, which he rightly affirms to be a singular, essentially Hebrew tradition, and the modern successors to the ancient Greeks. He illustrates the contrast with an anecdote from one of his Rabbi teachers who happened to be seated on a plane next to a key figure in the Israeli socialist movement.[3] The Rabbi had one of his students seated farther back in the plane—a young man who constantly attended to his needs, bringing him slippers because his feet would swell on long flights, bringing him sandwiches because he knew he disliked airline food. The socialist turned to the Rabbi and said, "I am so impressed with your son. I have four grown sons, but in all their life I don't remember any of them offering to do anything for me. Why is your son doing all this?"

The Rabbi replied, "He isn't my son. Had my son been here you would have really seen service. But don't blame yourself: your sons are faithful to your teachings and my sons are faithful to my teachings. You made the decision to teach your sons that you are descended from apes. That means that you are one generation closer to an ape than they, so it is only proper that you acknowledge their status and serve them. I chose to teach my sons that we came from God himself. That puts me one generation closer to the Ultimate Truth, which means it is only appropriate that they treat me accordingly." Ideas have consequences.

Assumptions about Life

Space will not permit the extensive treatment of a multitude of divergent presuppositions that lie beneath the Greek and Hebrew views of life. But these assumptions have huge ramifications. Let us mention some of the key areas and note where some practical implications for education become apparent:

1. Morality: How do we determine right from wrong?

For the Hebrew, man is not the measure of all things. Neither the individual conscience (as in Athens) nor the collective wisdom of public opinion (as in Sparta) could adequately guide human morality. Both the individual and the group were subject to a higher, objective authority. Reason is trumped by revelation. To what degree do our emphases, for example, on human freedom or people's opinions suggest a dependence on Greek assumptions? Where does this become apparent in the classroom?

2. Sinfulness: Is man inherently good or bad?

The Greeks had no consistent foundation for their view of the primacy of man (other than the "survival of the fittest"), yet in their commitment to "man as the measure of all things" they stressed the potentiality of man, either in a collectivist or an individualist sense. The Hebrews, in their understanding of man as a creature made in God's image, had a far more solid basis for human worth, but they also had a realistic assessment of man's frailty in the doctrine of the Fall. The biblical doctrine of "total depravity" affirms that every part of every man, including his thinking, has to some degree been spoiled by the consequences of sin; man's sinfulness has implications for his ability to learn.

Most educational theories fail to take into account the debilitating consequences of sin in the academic realm. The fall of man has affected our minds as well as our bodies. There is a sin component to learning disabilities. They are not necessarily a result of specific sins in the student, but in some measure all disabilities are a consequence of sin's intrusion in the world. There can be no solution to sin other than in the redemptive work of Christ experienced in the power of the Holy Spirit. Yet to what degree have we placed our faith in the Greek assumption that man's Reason remains untainted by sin, and thus really believe that there are educational answers to both behavioral and academic problems?

3. Family: What is the nature of the family?

For the Hebrews, the family was the basic building block of society; among the Greeks the basic building block was either the army barracks (in Sparta) or the individual (in Athens). For the Jews, this meant that all of life operated in a family way: the very nation considered itself as a family with a single father, Abraham. Similarly the church in the New Testament is viewed as a family ("Our Father," "brother in Christ," etc.).

Our models of school oscillate between the Spartan collectivist approach (submerge all students into a common system with a centrally determined curriculum) and an Athenian individualist approach (self-expression). How do we create a model of Christian education that embodies the relational dynamics of family? The danger of the Christian school is that it perpetrates the collectivist ideal of the State system, but the danger of home-schooling is that it reflects the individualism of Athens.

4. Parenting: To what degree is parenting directive?

Spartan parents had no say in the future of their children; they simply handed them over to the city-state where the experts took over. Athenian parents equally had no say; they simply pampered their children with games, toys, sports, and entertainment and allowed children to discover their own destiny. As the Athenian statesman Pericles put it, "Each single one of our citizens, in all the manifold aspects of life, is able to show himself the rightful lord and owner of his own person, and to do this, moreover with exceptional grace and exceptional versatility."[4]

In a Hebrew family, parental authority, and particularly patriarchal authority, was crucial both in instruction and direction (see for example Genesis 18:19). In education we need to understand that children need directive authority (*contra* Athens), but that directive authority is in the context of the need to "honor Father and Mother" (*contra* Sparta). Do we fall into Athenian or Spartan misunderstandings of the role of authority?

5. Youth: Is the younger generation the "hope for the future"?

Children were lovingly received in Hebrew families as entrustments from the Lord, and thus not discarded, as they so often were in Greece. But they were never viewed as the center of the home. They were trained to realize from the start that life did not revolve around them. In Greek culture, the children who survived grew up in a child-centered environment. Plutarch gives us a glimpse into the family of Themistocles, the general in charge of the Athenian army. He records Themistocles as saying that his son "who was pert toward his mother [...] wielded more power than anybody else in Greece." He based this on his own observation that the Athenians ruled the Greeks, he ruled the Athenians, the boy's mother ruled himself, and the boy ruled his mother![5]

Such a statement, even in jest, would have been shameful in Israel where it was considered a curse to be ruled by women and children. For ancient Israel, the hope of the future did not rest in the hands of youth, but on the shoulders of fathers and elders. If the younger generation was to walk into blessing, it was the fathers who would lead them there. Age was venerated. Each succeeding generation was not seeking its own identity (Baby boomers, Generation X, etc.). There were no youth movements, no youth cultures, no youth music styles, no youth churches. In what ways does our education system promote the distinctiveness of our young people and alienate them from their elders, their heritage, their traditions? Or how could it better serve a multi-generational harmony (Malachi 4:5)? Have we followed the example of the Boy Scouts who recently changed Baden-Powell's 75-year old declaration made by each wolf cub from "The cub gives in to the Old Wolf; the cub does not give in to himself" to "The Cub respects the Old Wolf; the Cub respects himself"?

6. Philosophy: Why were the Hebrews poor philosophers?

The Greeks, in their new-found capacity to reason, which had debunked the old beliefs in multitudinous gods, were on a quest to understand. But the Hebrews never had reason to doubt the reality of a personal God whose power had been seen by countless witnesses in their rich heritage. They had no need to question God's existence; their questions related to what He required of *their* existence. God had spoken. But, as Abram Sachar says in *A History of the Jews*, where the Hebrews asked, "What must I do?" the Greeks asked, "Why must I do it?" Or, as Abraham Heschel put it, "The Greeks learned in order to comprehend. The Hebrews learned in order to revere."[6] These contrasts raise immediate implications for the focus of educational endeavors.

Christian education in the Hebrew tradition focuses more on practical application in a context of obedience ("What must I do?") rather than on speculations in an abstract context. And Christian learning is a means to an end: to glorify God—an end of worship and an end of obedience—rather than an end in itself, learning to simply understand. Is it always helpful to encourage young children to ask "Why?" Is it not better to train a young child to obey—to instantly stand still when told to rather than running out into the road? Are not explanations more suited for those who have learned to obey without question (see John 7:17)?

7. Dualism: separating the material and non-material worlds.

Plato was one of the most famous Greek thinkers. In his search for truth, with his own reason as his starting point, he sought for unchanging universals, ideals that existed only in the non-material world. So, he pointed out, the idea of a circle exists as an ideal, but whenever it is drawn on a piece of paper it can only ever be an imperfect, or at least temporary, expression of that eternal ideal. The outcome of Plato's thought was a devaluing of the physical world and a mystical elevating of the unseen world of ideals.

But the Hebrews knew that, while there is a distinction between the temporal and the eternal, all that God has made in a material world is good, not secondary. The Jews not only affirmed the physical world, but also saw in that affirmation the positive value of physical work. Manual labor was beneath the dignity of the Greek philosophers, but the Hebrews had no such philosophers—all of their great thinkers were also doers: shepherds, tent-makers, etc. How much has Greek dualism infiltrated our Christian schools? Do we regard the Bible course as more spiritual than the science course? Do we gear our programs toward thinkers and have a lower estimation of those whose successes in life will be accomplished with their hands rather than their heads? Are we training our students to live and work in the real world?

8. Culture: What was it like to live in Hebrew or Greek communities?

In the Gospels we read of Jesus occasionally visiting the "Cities of the Decapolis." These were ten cities that had been deliberately built to create Greek cultures in Hebrew territories, perhaps in the hope that the Jewish people would become more assimilated into the Empire. Their central architectural features introduced three elements that had never previously been found in *any* Hebrew city: a sports arena, a theatre, and a public education facility. It is hard to imagine today even the smallest community being without facilities for sport, entertainment, and public education. But to the Hebrews these were entirely novel concepts, and while there is evidence in the teaching of Jesus and Paul of their awareness of these novelties, it remains clear that these cities in New Testament times were thought of as dark places. It is no coincidence that when Mark tells of the demoniac Legion, the story is told of Jesus going over to "*...the other side*" (Mark 5:1)—this man was a resident of the region of Decapolis, and it was there he was to remain to tell his story (Mark 5:19,20).

The Hebrews understood the importance of physical fitness, though the wildly popular sports of the day were not part of that. They had a rich culture: literature was profound; music was vibrant; artistry was skillful. Their art was very different than Greek sculptures, which gave solid expression to the Greek ideal of man as the measure of all things. But there were no theatres. Their educational system was very effective, though centered in the home and synagogue and with a vastly different curriculum than that of the public institutions. Surely we should ask how much the world has become the model for what we consider to be normal life? Has Christian education brought light into the darkness of the Decapolis, or has the Decapolis blinded the Church with its invading darkness?

What does Hebrew Education Look Like?

Since the days of the Renaissance, modern humanism has made great progress. It is clear that there are significant similarities between modern thought in humanistic education and ancient Greek philosophy. Paul Kurtz, professor of philosophy at the State University of New York and a major contributor to the Humanist Manifesto II, honestly claimed, "Our model is not Moses, Jesus, or Mohammed, but Socrates."[7] But history teaches us that the Roman Empire could not survive, built as it was on Greek assumptions—it was one of those structures of which Jesus predicted total collapse if built on any other foundation than His truth.

In our day we are also witnessing the cracks appearing in the structure of the modern educational empire. It is not so much that the system is failing; rather, it is that the system is arriving at the logical conclusion of its underlying assumptions. Life without God does not work properly. There is an important management principle that states: "Your system is perfectly designed to produce the results you are getting." The modern educational system is designed to produce the results that it is getting. Ideas have consequences, and just as the consequences of Greek assumptions were seen in the fall of the Roman Empire, so they are now being seen in the crumbling of modern education. It is time to revisit the Hebrew model!

In Sparta, education, as theologian William Barclay pointed out, was for "the obliteration of the individual in the service of the State."[8] It was different in Athens where the individual was anything but obliterated. Schools pampered the individual and were almost entirely free from public regulation. The focus was on literature, music, and gymnastics, and, as Barclay put it, education was for "the training of the individual in the service of culture." But among the Jews, Barclay characterized education as "the training of the individual in the service of God."

The Bible says very little about schools directly, but it has much to say about learning, pupils, and teachers. The biblical model for learning begins with the family, where parents have the responsibility of training up self-governing individuals to be released to serve God in the world. We cannot hope to see any significant improvement in our schools unless this foundation is in place. Parents prepare their children for learning, training them in basic skills like listening when an adult is speaking, honoring the one giving instruction, obeying promptly, and controlling oneself. It is almost hopeless to expect teachers in school to inculcate these skills if their opposites have already been trained into being by the time the child is sent to school. These are the foundational skills that must be established in the home prior to formal education. Without families functioning in this way we cannot ultimately change what happens in schools.

But the Hebrew model does not stop with individual families. The Jews were a community-minded people, and education took place in a community of like-minded families with a commonly held world-view, mutually applied standards of parenting, and agreed upon goals of learning. If it is hard to find families who prepare their children adequately for formal education, it is even harder to find communities of such families!

The community was not simply a matter of like-minded parents. Those parents would only entrust their children to like-minded teachers, for any teacher outside of the home was to be viewed as a representative of the father himself. The parents would not have asked of a potential teacher, "What kind of scholar is he?" but rather, "What kind of person is he?" They recognized, as we have seen, that a pupil would not simply become a younger version of a head full of similar facts, but would actually become like his teacher (Luke 6:40). Like-minded parents hire like-minded teachers whom they would not hesitate to have their children imitate.

Within such a community, like-mindedness will affirm a singular goal for learning. According to Proverbs, the principle aim of learning is to gain wisdom and understanding (Proverbs 4:7). But this is not the wisdom against which Paul took aim in 1 Corinthians. Hebrew wisdom has nothing to do with intellectual skills or abstract speculations. It is quite possible to be "smart" without being wise in the Hebrew sense. In the pursuit of smartness, many have succeeded in becoming educated fools. A respected Jewish author, Abraham Heschel, defined his people's view of wisdom as "the ability to look at things from the point of view of God." Clearly this is different to Greek wisdom: "Know thyself!" was Socrates' cry, but the cry of the Hebrews was "Know God!" With that insight, the Jews were equipped to know what to do in the world with what they had learned, for wisdom had to do with the appropriate application of knowledge.

In this we see that the Hebrew model of education rests upon a moral base, not an academic one. Knowledge apart from virtue is vanity. That is not to say that intellectual pursuits do not have their place, nor that academic excellence is unimportant. But it recognizes that, as Overman puts it, "Where virtue is laid as a foundation to knowledge, it is remarkable how much knowledge will actually be found! In an environment where students practice principles of self-government (i.e. self-control) not only can a teacher accomplish a great deal of teaching, but students can accomplish a great deal of learning."[9]

ENDNOTES

1. Quoted by Overman: Assumptions that affect our lives (Chatsworth CA: Micah 6:8 ; 1996) p.45

2. ibid p.51

3. Rabbi Daniel Lapin: America's Real War (Sisters OR: Multnomah; 1999) p.51f

4. Quoted by Overman, op cit p.63

5. ibid p.124f

6. Quoted by Overman, op cit p.148

7. ibid p.243

8. ibid p.219f

9. ibid p.226

Part 5

The Authority of our Curriculum:

Christian Education Teaches All of God's Word
for All of Life

Chapter 9

Giving up the Bible

Where do we start in building a curriculum? Secular schools start with the Department of Education curriculum guide. Christian education starts with the Bible. We will end up covering most of the same subject matter, but if our starting point is different, then what we do with that subject matter will be radically different.

The Bible anticipates that this will be our approach, for rather than viewing knowledge as unrelated to spiritual reality, it declares that *"The fear of the LORD is the beginning of knowledge"* (Proverbs 1:7). That is to say, we start our journey toward understanding on the premise that we hold God in awe as the One who knows all there is to know about everything. What He says on any subject determines what is important about that subject. At the heart of the matter is the question of authority: is autonomous man free to chart his own course of study and come to his own conclusions about reality, or is man, as a finite creature before his Creator, responsible to God and dependent on His revelation?

Christians may generally agree that God is authoritative in the areas in which He speaks, but there is much disagreement as to what He speaks about. At some level, all Christians receive the Bible as the Word of God. But most would question the extent to which that Word addresses many of the issues that take up most of our time in school. Cornelius Van Til said, "The Bible is authoritative on everything to which it speaks. And it speaks of everything."[1] Does "everything" really mean *everything*? Few would go that far. They may assent to the first half of Van Til's statement ("The Bible is authoritative on *everything to which it speaks*"); but they would pull back from the implications of the second half ("It speaks *of everything*"). They may receive God's Word as authoritative on such matters as morality or spirituality, but would balk at the prospect of embracing its ultimate authority in matters of geology or biology, music or math, civics or physics.

Ken Ham and his organization "Answers in Genesis"[2] have been at the forefront of a movement to try to awaken the church to the implications of centuries of erosion in her foundations concerning the authority of the Word of God. Ham refers to Gallup polls revealing the shift that has occurred. In 1963, two out of three Americans told Gallup they believed "the Bible is the actual Word of God and is to be taken literally, word for word." By 1998, only one in three took that stance, while nearly half preferred: "The Bible is the inspired Word of God, not everything in it should be taken literally."[3]

Taking the Bible Literally

The debate, of course, is over what is meant by "literally." Few would argue that when, in quoting Psalm 23, we say, *"He makes me to lie down in green pastures,"* we are expecting the Lord, our shepherd, to rugby-tackle us in a field. We understand that the psalm is using poetic language. All would agree that the meaning depends on the type of literature involved. But when churches claim to take God's Word "seriously but not literally" there is usually more at stake.

While in Psalms the intent of the author was clearly poetic, in other instances the context suggests that the writer is speaking factually. So, for example, the book of Genesis is written in a narrative, historical style rather than a poetic form of literature, or a style that bears any resemblance to the mythological accounts of origins in other religions' holy books. New Testament writers clearly believe that Old Testament writers are to be understood factually. Jesus speaks of Jonah as really being in a fish, Peter speaks of a global flood really happening, and Paul speaks of Eve really being formed subsequently to and distinctly from Adam. These three stories alone address, among other things, important matters of history, geology and anthropology. This means, to apply Van Til's statement, that in speaking of everything, the Bible speaks of such things as history, geology, and anthropology. Where it addresses such matters it is to be received authoritatively.

This represents a distinctly different view of the Bible than is now common in most churches. As Ken Ham points out, such things as Jonah and the great fish, Noah's Ark, and the Garden of Eden are talked about. But they are treated as "Bible stories." Gradually, the distinction between story and history, between fable and fact becomes blurred. They are great stories, stories filled with all kinds of spiritual meanings. But it has become less and less clear whether they are to be taken as "literally" true. So, as Ham puts it:

Most Sunday school and Christian school literature concentrates on teaching Bible stories. Now these stories are important [...] But this is what is happening today: in our churches we teach Bible *stories*—Jonah and the whale—Jesus' death and resurrection—the feeding of the five thousand—Noah's ark—and so on. But the children then go out into the world. Most go to public schools, watch secular television, and read newspapers and magazines. And what is the world saying to them? That you can't trust the Bible. Science has proved the Bible wrong, they say.[4]

We keep telling the stories, but increasingly they are reduced to the level of fairy tales and received as such.

It used to be that such a problem only existed in the so-called liberal churches. But this approach to the Word of God is now more widespread, as seen in a book called *The Message of Genesis*, written by Ralph H. Elliot, and published by the Southern Baptist's Sunday School Board (and thus indicative of the approach to Bible stories in more conservative circles). Elliot writes:

One can say with [Alan] Richardson: "We must learn to think of the stories of Genesis—the creation, the Fall, Noah's ark, the Tower of Babel [...] in the same way that we think of the parables of Jesus; they are profoundly symbolical (although not allegorical) stories, which aren't to be taken as literally true."[5]

The flaw in his argument, however, is that Jesus clearly described his parables as parables so that nobody was ever under the illusion that they were anything other than stories. Moses, however, wrote as fact, and his accounts were understood as factual by Jesus and the New Testament writers. We must understand parables as parables and poetry as poetry. But where a passage has all the hallmarks of being intended to be understood literally, then we must treat it as such. In fact, it must be treated as authoritative on the subjects it deals with, and as the starting point for our thinking on such subjects.

Does it Matter?

Many would argue that in wanting to defend the historicity and reliability of Old Testament Bible "stories" we are majoring on minors. Surely we ought to focus our energy on the proclamation of the gospel. After all, it is surely not necessary to salvation that one believes in a literal 6-day creation or a global flood. But as Ham and his colleagues have so ably demonstrated, the erosion of the foundation of the authority of the Bible has had a far more significant impact on the gospel than we have realized. In fact, Christianity has consistently been on the decline in the wake of these trends. While the following matters are dealt with much more thoroughly in the *Answers in Genesis* materials, we take time here simply to note some of the implications:

> * If we cannot trust the history of the Old Testament, why would we expect people to trust the history of the New Testament? We maintain that Christianity is an historical faith, based on the historical facts of Jesus' death and bodily resurrection. As Paul says, if there is no resurrection, our faith is in vain. But how do we know that there is a resurrection? Only on the basis of an historical narrative in the Word of God. We get angry when others treat the account of the resurrection as a "spiritual story," denying the physical resurrection of our Lord Jesus. But what is the literary difference between Moses' account of the Flood and Mark's account of the Resurrection? If the historicity of one is in question, it is inevitable that the historicity of the other will be doubted.

* If the Bible is unreliable as a guide to our understanding of anthropology, why would we expect people to trust it as a guide to our morality? For example, all that we believe about the sanctity of marriage is rooted in the biblical account of Adam and Eve. Both Jesus (Mark 10:1-8) and Paul (1 Corinthians 11:8-12) derive the authority for their teaching about marriage from the account in Genesis. Marriage as the union of a man and a woman able to become one flesh is based on the fact that God made the woman from the man. If marriage began when a descendant from an ape-man took a liking to a descendant from an ape-woman, then choosing a partner is entirely a matter of preference (man, woman, or whatever), and the institution of marriage is nothing more than a social convention that may change with the times.

* If the Bible only speaks of "spiritual" things, often in the form of stories with a moral, then where do we go for our understanding of the real world? The answer has become only too apparent. Children are sent to Sunday School to learn their spiritual lessons; then they go to a "proper" school to learn about the things that really matter. And of course, the public school system is happy to oblige with its own theories that become accepted as the truth on such matters as science and society. Along the way, the Bible is mocked for its presentation on such issues, and within a generation or two even the spiritual truths lose their appeal. If they have no basis in fact, they have no more authority than the experiential mysticism of alternative spiritualities with which many people are replacing them. Sadly, the Church has been happy to settle for this poor deal in which we have the right to influence in the spiritual matters so long as we leave the real world to the humanists. We get heaven and they get the earth.

* If the Bible is inaccurate in its depiction of the origins of death, then it is not to be trusted in its solution to our final enemy. The Old Testament makes two fundamental assertions that the New Testament builds upon in the proclamation of the gospel.

Firstly, that we sin as descendants of Adam, carrying in our beings the hereditary consequences of his sin. That, in turn, is compounded by our own history of sin. In response to this Jesus came as the Second Adam with a salvation specifically geared to solving the problems of Adam's race. His work would have no relevance to any supposed descendants of other pre-historic, man-like creatures.

Secondly, if death existed millions of years before man, in a fossil record that is supposed to pre-date man but which shows evidence not only of death, but of disease (dinosaurs with cancer) and thorns (which the Bible states to be the consequence of the Fall), then we have to conclude that death is a result of God's creative failings rather than a consequence of man's sin. If it was God who caused the death and suffering in the world, which is the implication of a view that death appears in the annals of history prior to the fall of man, we are without hope. In that case, even if Jesus' death earned forgiveness for men's sins it would have been of no value in solving the problems of a dying creation. But if it was man's sin that unleashed death and destruction onto the human race and the rest of the created order, then in dealing with sin, Jesus really has opened up the prospect of a new heaven and earth in which there is no more suffering.

Thus if we spiritualize away the historicity of the Genesis account of the Garden of Eden, we end up with no basis for the gospel which was specifically designed to deal with the problem described in the Garden. No garden, no gospel. Without Adam we have no second Adam. Without the Garden law of sin and death (the principle that the two must go hand-in-hand: sin leads to death, and death is the consequence of sin), there is no guarantee that dealing with sin will make any difference to the problem of death, for if death existed before sin was present, there would be no reason to expect that it cannot exist after sin has been done away with.

We may choose to ignore "minor" issues like the various theories of creation and the origins of social institutions like marriage or nations. We may argue that these are really less important than the heart of the gospel message about trusting in Jesus and saving souls. But when we lose confidence in the Bible's authority in these secondary matters, there is much more at stake, for we find that a foundation has been eroded and we end up losing even the primary matters.

The gospel did not appear in a vacuum. God spent thousands of years in human history and divine revelation preparing for its coming. It was only "...*when the fullness of time had come*" that God sent His Son (Galatians 4:4). Without all that precedes, the gospel is foolishness, which is why, when Paul was proclaiming the gospel to pagans who had no sense of that historical context, he began with Genesis (see Acts 17:22-28). Truly Genesis is named as a book of beginnings—not merely the beginnings of the universe or the human race, but the foundational beginnings of every Christian doctrine, every issue of Christian morality, and every branch of Christian knowledge and learning.

In *How Now Shall we Live*, Charles Colson wrote:

Christian education is not simply a matter of starting class with Bible reading and prayer, then teaching subjects out of secular textbooks. It consists of teaching everything, from science and mathematics to literature and the arts, within the framework of an integrated biblical worldview. It means teaching students to relate every academic discipline to God's truth and his self-revelation in Scripture, while detecting and critiquing non-biblical worldview assumptions.[6]

But where do we go to find what an "integrated biblical worldview" looks like? In particular, where in the Bible do we find a framework within which to understand the kinds of specifics that Colson lists: science and mathematics, literature and the arts? It is not the kind of question that evangelicals have been accustomed to ask, for we do not see Jesus saying a great deal about science or mathematics; Paul shows a knowledge of literature but says very little about a framework within which to understand the arts.

Because Jesus and Paul in particular do not have much to say about such subjects, we have assumed that these issues are relatively unimportant. Surely what matters are grand biblical themes like salvation and God's purpose for the church. The New Testament is where we are most at home. The Old Testament is read with a quaint interest in the background leading up to the New Testament, but with a measure of suspicion, as we know we have somehow left the old covenant and now live under grace not law. Yet Ken Ham has taken us back to the book of beginnings, and we, with him, are arguing that if that Old Testament foundation is lost, we will end up losing the New Testament too!

If we do not start at the beginning, we find there is no end: the gospel itself begins to disintegrate without the foundation that the Old Testament revelation provides. But all that we learn in every other area of life is equally fragile. As we shall see in our next chapter, Christian educators must rediscover the Old Testament.

ENDNOTES

1. Cornelius Van Til: The Defence of the Faith, (Philadelphia: Presbyterian & Reformed Publishing; 1967) p.8

2. For information on this ministry and the materials it produces, see www.AnswersinGenesis.org

3. Web-site Article: "Bruce Willis and the Gallup Poll—an alarming trend" (www.AnswersinGenesis.org)

4. Ken Ham: Why won't they listen? (Green Forest AR: Master Books; 2002) p.88

5. Quoted by Ham: op cit p.89

6. Charles Colson & Nancy Pearcey: How now shall we live? (Wheaton: Tyndale; 1999) p.338

Chapter 10

Rediscovering the Old Testament

In a book on Christian education, it seems strange to focus on the Book of Genesis. The pole to which the magnet of the church's attention shifts is understandably the New Testament. With the commendable emphasis on the message of the gospel to "Trust in Jesus," the Old Testament has come to seem somewhat superfluous.

There are theological reasons for the intensifying of that shift in recent decades. The pervasive influence of dispensationalism has rendered the Old Testament largely irrelevant; many Christians have come to see it as relating only to a previous era. In this mindset, it not only relates to a by-gone age historically, but also to a dispensation that is both different to and actually in conflict with our own time, for now we live in the age of grace. In such thinking, the Old Testament only has appeal as a reminder of the way things used to be, over-arched by a great sense of relief that that is not the ways things are now. It is seen as a book of stories, with moral lessons to be learned, but not much more. And the pietistic interpretation of grace as being essentially a matter of personal and internal religious experience further distances us from the Old Testament, for there we see a big sweep of history in which individuals were but a small part of movements that encompassed entire nations. Personal salvation does not seem to figure prominently in the Old Testament.

Where do we go to get Equipped as Teachers?

We considered Charles Colson's desire to approach academic subjects "within the framework of an integrated biblical worldview." That must start with an integrated approach to the whole Bible. It is only when we have taken into account all that the Bible says on any subject that we will be able to have a view of the Bible's true teaching on that subject. We need Genesis as much as John. In 2 Timothy 3:16 and 17, Paul insisted that *"ALL Scripture is given by inspiration of God"* (emphasis added).

Of course, when he was writing, it was the Old Testament scriptures that he had in mind. So, our integrated biblical worldview must integrate the entirety of God's inspired revelation. Paul goes on to say that this entire body of revelation is profitable so that "the man of God may be complete, thoroughly equipped for EVERY good work" (emphasis added). ALL of Scripture equips for EVERY good work. If we take the whole Bible, we may have a complete worldview, one that addresses every issue of human activity. Our human activities, be they in prayer meetings or business meetings, will only truly be good works if they are equipped and informed by the revelation of the whole of Scripture as pertaining to those activities. It will take an overview of the whole Bible to have a worldview that adequately informs our thinking in the areas where we work, if that work is to be good work.

We have noted that in ancient times, a pre-requisite for anybody who was about to become a king was that they must first write out in their own hand a copy of the Law (Deuteronomy 17:18). In this way the new monarch was to be "thoroughly equipped for every good work" in his responsibilities as king. This would also be a useful exercise for those of us who are not planning to become kings. We have a different set of "good works" that God has prepared beforehand for us to walk in (Ephesians 2:10). Perhaps those whose calling is in Christian education, as parents, teachers, or administrators, could similarly prepare themselves for their "good works" in the realm of education. They could plan to read the whole Bible, underlining in various colored pencils all that they can find that relates to such subjects as "teaching," "learning," "the child," and the particular academic disciplines that they are responsible to teach.

If we were to undertake such a project, it would be an interesting exercise to do a statistical analysis of where in the Bible we found the most relevant references. To some degree, these samplings would take us out of the areas of the Bible with which we are most familiar. While the pages of our Bible might look predominantly red in the Gospels, for the publisher chose to highlight the words of Jesus in red ink, we may find surprisingly few underlinings in our other colored crayons there, compared with other parts of the Bible. Sure, there would be lots of verses underlined in the Gospels if we were doing a search for prayer or faith; but how many for science or art?

This is where we face a crucial issue of biblical interpretation. If the New Testament says very little on a subject, does that mean that this subject is somehow not really important? This has been the basis for some to say that Christians should not be overly concerned about the realm of politics, for Jesus and Paul talked about personal salvation and the life of the church, but never told us to run for election as a public official, nor even to try to put pressure on the government to change its policies.

Many Things are Hardly Mentioned in the New Testament

It is true that the New Testament says relatively little about politics. But is that because politics are relatively unimportant? I suggest not. Rather, the New Testament says little about politics because the Old Testament has already said a lot! The New Testament has much to say about that which is "new," so there we see an emphasis on wonderful truths like the new birth, salvation in Christ, and the Church. But it does not need to repeat what is already familiar.

The Old Testament, on the other hand, devotes whole books to the issue of politics. What are the Books of Kings if not God's worldview of what goes on in the government of nations? The Law of Moses outlines God's instructions for how a nation is to be governed, the history books chronicle how nations were actually governed, and the prophets give God's report cards for each government in light of what He had required of them. There is no shortage of material with which to come to our conclusions about a biblical worldview of government. But most of it appears in the Old Testament.

It is at this point that many start to get nervous. We have tended to believe that since the old has been done away with, we only retain in the New Covenant era that which is reiterated in the New Testament. Thus for example, Christians continue to believe in prayer, because an Old Testament theme is pursued and developed in the New Testament. But many no longer see the need to practice tithing because that particular law is not restated as law, even though it is still referred to in the New Testament. There are, however, numerous ethical issues that are not explicitly restated in the New Testament. To take an extreme example, bestiality is explicitly forbidden in the Old Testament but not in the New. Yet surely the Lord assumes that we are so persuaded of the abhorrence of such a practice on the basis of what He has already said in the Old Testament that we need no further reinforcement in the New Testament.

Jesus said that He had not come to abolish the Law but to fulfill it. Moral prohibitions remain in force unless they are explicitly repealed in the New Testament. We recognize that there is a refining process in the progressive revelation throughout the centuries in which that revelation was transmitted. But it is God who does the refining. Unless He adjusts His instructions for life, they remain in effect. The fact that they are recorded in the Old Testament rather than the New Testament does not change that.

Some subjects, like civil government, are dealt with much more fully in the Old Testament. We must be willing to submit our thinking on any subject to the entirety of God's revealed Word on that subject. His Word is the starting point for our thinking and establishes the boundaries within which our thinking may proceed. And in many instances, that Word is largely spelled out in the Old Testament. At the very least, the beginnings of our knowledge of a biblical worldview start in the Old Testament, and often in the first eleven chapters of Genesis in particular.

Starting at the "Beginning"

Genesis is a book of beginnings. It is here that we face our first challenge as to whether we are going to subject our thinking to God's wisdom and revelation. Conelius Van Til wrote: "The question of knowledge is an ethical question."[1] It is in Adam that we see the origins of man's calling to know. He was instructed to "name" the creatures in the process of developing knowledge in order to subdue and use the earth under God and to God's glory. What he knew and how he knew was part of his relationship as a creature before his Creator. But his understanding and his knowledge became warped the moment that he stepped into rebellion. His rebellion had little to do with eating a piece of fruit. It was all to do with questioning what God had said, and wanting to know for himself rather than submitting his understanding to what God had revealed.

As R.J. Rushdoony puts it, "Man in rebellion against God is in rebellion against the very foundation of all true knowledge, and this fact must be basic to Christian education. No neutrality is possible, because there are no neutral facts in the universe, only God-created facts. Men either accept God's interpretation, or they attempt as their own gods to create their own universe of meaning."[2] This was the war being waged in the Garden of Eden as Adam and Eve succumbed to the temptation to be as gods, to set themselves up as judges of God's revealed description of the universe (*"Has God indeed said?"*—Genesis 3:1). They wanted to make up their own minds as to how to interpret reality (*"...[to be] like God"*—Genesis 3:5).

It is no easier for us today to subject our thinking on any subject to the scrutiny of God's Word than it was for Adam. We have been programmed to think that God's Word has nothing significant to say outside of the so-called spiritual realm. But if we say, with Colson, that we want to teach "everything, from science and mathematics to literature and the arts, within the framework of an integrated biblical worldview," we have a huge challenge. This entails far more than Colson says when he continues that this "means teaching students to relate every academic discipline to God's truth and His self-revelation in Scripture." The hard part is not in teaching students to relate every academic discipline to God's truth in Scripture; far harder is learning as parents and Christian teachers to bring *our own* thinking about those subjects under the microscope of God's Word.

If we say that we want to teach from an integrated biblical world-view, this implies that we have been able to start to measure all that we think against the yardstick of the Word of God. We acknowledge it to be the standard by which all truth is measured. Recognizing the need for a biblical worldview implies that we want to view the world—the real world, not just spirituality and the life of the Church—through the lens of the Bible. The Bible becomes the standard of measurement to which all of our thinking is to be subjected.

In all of our judgments about what is right or good or true, we need a standard. Have you ever tried to draw a straight line without a standard, such as a ruler, to follow? As good as your line initially seemed as you put pencil to paper, when you placed your line up against a straight edge, the line was clearly crooked. Or have you tried to determine the exact length of something by simple eyeball inspection? The only way to be sure that our assessment is accurate is when we use a proper standard of measurement. Such standards are needed in all our thinking. Developing a biblical worldview is the process of acknowledging that our own attempts at thinking need to be measured by an absolute standard that exists outside of our fallen selves. That standard is the Bible.

But, many would complain, surely the Bible does not say enough about most of the complex academic subjects that we are exploring with our students? Surely we would have very little to teach if our biology textbook was no more than a few related Bible verses?

Of course, the Bible does not purport to be a textbook on all the academic disciplines; indeed it does not claim to say *much* about any of those disciplines. But, in stating that "all scripture is [...] profitable [...] for every good work," it does claim that it says *enough* about each subject for us to be able, by God's grace, to pursue our studies in a way that is true and reflective of God's purposes in that realm. God has not said all that there is to say about any subject. He chose to give us the adventure of being able to explore the infinite with our finite minds. This is the privilege of a lifetime, and perhaps an eternity, spent in learning all that there is to learn! But he has said enough about each subject to ensure that we know all that we *need* to know. He has given us a map so that we don't get lost in our explorations unless we choose to ignore the map. And as every wife knows, men would rather find their own way than look at a map or ask for directions!

The Beginning of Knowledge

The Bible uses the phrase, "the *beginning* of knowledge." Knowledge has a starting point, the underlying principle on which all is to be built. The Bible tells us enough about every subject to know where to start and the legitimate direction of our studies. It gives us enough of the big picture to know when we are getting outside of our legitimate mandate to know and to subdue the earth to God's glory. We have been led to believe that the Bible only teaches religion, and that secular schools teach real life subjects like science, mathematics, and literature. But we cannot escape the fact that the Bible teaches about such things too. The only question is whether what the Bible says about them or what the schools say about them is accurate. They are saying very different things.

Ken Ham puts it this way: "[T]he history recorded from the beginning in the Bible does involve issues of biology, geology, astronomy, anthropology and chemistry. Now the Bible is not a science textbook (which is a good thing, since science textbooks change every year!). But the Bible is a revelation of history that gives us the 'Big Picture' in every area of reality. In other words, the Bible gives us the right foundational thinking so we can approach geology, biology, anthropology, etc. in the correct way."[3]

The Old Testament, and Genesis in particular, is so important because it is the starting point for our thinking. We know that what God says is true, so we start first with what He says about each subject. Consider the implications of this for our approach to some of the areas of our curriculum:

* The Bible tells us that death entered the world after, and as a result of, sin. That becomes our starting point for such disciplines as geology and paleontology. Our observations tell us that the earth is covered with rocks full of fossils—dead things. Since death came after the fall of man, they cannot pre-date that event. We therefore need to look for an alternative explanation. How can we account for all this evidence of death? The Bible leads us to a conclusion that fits the facts. It speaks of a global flood. As Ham puts it, if such an event had occurred we would expect to see "billions of dead things buried in rock layers laid down by water all over the earth." Which, of course, is what we see.

* The Bible tells us that God created distinct "kinds" of animals and plants to reproduce after their own kind. That is our starting point for biology. The world tells us that ancient animals and plants evolved into radically different kinds and higher forms of life. But our observations show us something else. Mutations and natural selections adapting to a new environment reveal a *downhill* change. They do not lead to more complex life forms. They merely show us how complex information coding

for great engineering design is being *corrupted* or *lost* over time. The grand-scale theory of evolution—that microbes have become millipedes, magnolias, and microbiologists—demands that huge amounts of new information, of true genetic novelty, have arisen over millions of years. To show such new information arising from natural processes is the real challenge for evolutionists, and one for which they have no answer.[4] We observe, as the Bible stated, distinct kinds remaining as kinds.

* The Bible tells us that God created Adam and Eve, a real man and a real woman, and that all human beings are descended from them. That is our starting point for anthropology. There is only one race: the human race. The world wrestles with the supposed problem of racism, on the assumption that various "races" evolved separately and are allegedly at different stages of evolution. As is well known, the full title of Darwin's Magnum Opus was *Origin of the Species by means of Natural Selection, or the Preservation of the Favored Races in the Struggle for Life.* His theories of "races" (favored or less favored) have created the philosophical foundation for racist policies and attitudes for over a century, with devastating consequences.

But most evolutionists are now coming to the conclusion that the people groups did not have separate origins and did not evolve from separate animals. They are forced to accept the Creationist position that all people groups have come from the same original population. Many racist atrocities built on the assumption of one race being inferior to another would have been avoided if we had kept our thinking based on the biblical starting point and binding principle of anthropology. The Bible's account of varied people groups starts at the Tower of Babel. This offers the most reasonable explanation for the variety of ethnic groups that now exist and provides a perfectly adequate time frame for the distinctions to appear. Different groups became separated from a wider gene pool, and those whose skin color was best suited to the environment in which they settled became the dominant group within the limited local gene pool. If we start with the Bible, and live within its boundaries, we may avoid all kinds of hardship.

* The Bible tells us that marriage originated with God's creation of a man and woman: Adam and Eve, not Adam and Bruce (as Ken Ham, an Australian, points out). That is our starting point for sociology. Despite the attempts of modern educators to make the idea of a child with two fathers appear "normal" in cute elementary picture books, our "norm" (the true definition of normality) is fixed by the measuring stick in Genesis. If we discard the reliability of God's account of our origins, sociology is free to construct its own norms of social institutions. The Bible is not only clear on the origins of the family, it also speaks of the origins of the city, of culture, and of nations. With these fixed reference points, it also sets the parameters for life within these institutions, which it declares to be the handiwork of God, rather than an arbitrary construct suited to some stage of evolutionary development, but later to be discarded as irrelevant.

There are, of course, countless other matters of academic interest where the starting point will radically determine what is believed in the development of that discipline. Our goal here is merely to highlight our responsibility as Christian educators, whether as teachers in Christian schools or as parents assembling a learning program for home-schooled children. If we are to teach within the framework of a biblical worldview, we must ensure that we really do start with the Bible. The facts that we have to deal with are the same facts that everybody else has to handle, whether they are facts of history, astronomy, or archaeology. Our task is to develop theories to interpret those facts consistently with the biblical revelation. Biblical scholarship is true to God's Word, but it also offers explanations that are consistent with the evidence.

The endless cycle of discarding old theories and proposing new theories in every academic discipline (as yesterday's textbooks are rejected with disdain) is a sure testimony to the reality that autonomous human beings have no grasp of absolute truth in any of these areas. God is the only One who has the right to claim knowledge of absolute truth.

God's response to the theories of Job's comforters as they attempted to understand what was going on in their personal world is as telling today as it ever was. Whether we are trying to give an explanation of the origins of the world or of the human condition, God's challenge stands:

Where were you when I laid the foundations of the earth? (Job 38:4)

The rest of that chapter in Job is a devastating critique of the limitations of human understanding. It declares that all is the creative handiwork of God, that He is the only One who was present when the design was conceived. He alone sees in totality all of the events that have occurred in time and space, so His is the only interpretation of reality to be taken seriously! Science takes pride in its dependence on observation. God was the only one to observe the momentous events of creation; why would we not trust the only eye-witness account? He is the only One with the complete knowledge about any other facet of academic enquiry.

Defending the Authority of God's Word

God's interpretation of reality is the only one that matters. But this assumes that He has been able to communicate His interpretation accurately. And that, of course, is the heart of the matter. As the serpent put it at the beginning of time, *"Has God indeed said?"* (Genesis 3:1). Is God able to communicate? Is what He is purported to have said reliable? Is His Word authoritative?

A biblical worldview assumes a positive answer to these questions. If we have doubts in this regard, we will not be effectively teaching from a biblical worldview. We may be quoting selected Bible verses, but that alone is inadequate. So, to use Colson's phrase, how are parents to know if the teachers who are instructing their children are truly "teaching everything, from science and mathematics to literature and the arts, within the framework of an integrated biblical worldview"?

It will not be enough to simply know that those teachers are sitting in church every Sunday. Their doubts about whether God has truly spoken on all the subjects that are explored every day in school will probably not surface in the context of a Bible study in a religious setting. In that context, all good evangelicals are happy to affirm that they believe the Bible to be God's Word. But the doubts will appear when we talk about issues relating to the real world, and in particular the areas where teachers have become "experts" filled with the ideas of men. It is in the academic disciplines where, as they are about to teach science or history, the serpent whispers in their ear, *"Has God really said?"* At moments like that, we all have to choose whether to start our thinking with the theories we have been taught or with the clear statements of God's Word.

This challenge is the modern, sophisticated strategy of satan to do exactly what he was doing in a less subtle way with Adam and Eve in the Garden. The tragedy is that his tactics have worked in the Church as much as in the world. We have now reached the point where only 9% of U.S. teenagers who call themselves born again Christians believe there is such a thing as absolute truth.[5] Most have answered the serpent's question ("Has God really said?") with a resounding "No!"

How have so many reached this point? Since these teenagers claim to be "born again," we can probably assume that most have them have not been actively taught in their churches that there is no such thing as absolute truth. So where did this belief come from?

No Beginning, no End

It is perhaps no coincidence that 80-90% of students from church homes in America (probably higher in other countries) still attends public schools.[6] It is there that they are taught that God's Word cannot be trusted. Its history is ridiculed as they are taught that the earth is billions of years old, that man evolved from ape-like ancestors. They are persuaded that the Bible has nothing to do with science. If it appears to, its statements are erroneous, for it was the "big bang" that brought the earth into existence. The Bible, they are told, teaches religion, but schools teach real science and real history.

Having reached the point that most Christian teenagers mistrust the Bible's history, many of them are now beginning to question its reliability on moral issues. For many, their lifestyles are barely different from those of their non-Christian peers. This is visible in the movies they watch, the music they listen to, the way they dress, and the priorities that motivate their choices. The Barna Research Group released a significant finding in 2002. Among other statistics in a study entitled "Survey Shows Faith Impacts some Behaviors not Others"[7], they reported that there was no difference in behavior between churched and unchurched people in relation to reading a magazine or watching a video that contained explicit sexual images. Twenty percent of adults in both groups had done so in the past seven days.

But the erosion of biblical foundations is reaching its ultimate and intended conclusion: having doubted the Bible's history and then having doubted its morality, many Christian teenagers are now coming to the place of doubting its message of salvation. The Barna Research group now estimates that nearly 70% of young people who have been raised in Christian homes but attended public leave the church upon leaving home.[8]

Perhaps this will finally awaken the church to the problem. Many pastors have been happy to leave the real world to the humanists, provided they still had the corner on the market for spirituality. They were even unwilling to strongly address issues of morality such as sexuality, abortion, provocative dress, and popular culture among young people. Sin and repentance have not been high on the agenda in most pulpits. Issues of morality that get too close to home have often been avoided on the basis that it was good that these young people were at least in church to hear the message of the gospel, so nothing should be said that would frighten them away. Styles and standards have all been adjusted to accommodate young people. But those young people are leaving in droves anyway.

If 70% of the young people raised as Christians but educated in secular schools leave the church as soon as they are free to do so, surely we ought to be looking at alternative forms of education! It is not enough to learn Bible stories in church. It is not even enough to know the Bible's standards of morality. It is our task to demonstrate that the Bible can be trusted on all that it says about all of life. If our young people are persuaded of that fact, then they will receive the good news of the gospel unquestioningly and seek to live all of their life to the glory of God. Today's youth cannot live with the hypocrisy of a spiritual life that affects a religious component but is divorced from everyday reality.

Sadly, the statistics also suggest that the number of graduates of Christian schools who stop attending church when they leave school is also rising. This should not be a surprise: more and more of those schools are adopting the world's viewpoint on the Bible's essential unreliability on academic matters. It is almost inevitable that their students will then reject the Bible as God's authoritative Word on morality (as seen in the increasing prevalence of drug-related and sexual problems in Christian schools), and begin to doubt its message of salvation.

Our task is to give a resounding "Yes!" to answer the question of the serpent: *"Has God indeed said?"* He has spoken. He has spoken on all that we need to know about all of life. And what He has spoken is true. He has spoken in His Word, and from beginning to end His Word is to be received as authoritative, though with our finite minds we will not be able to comprehend all that it covers nor understand all that it says. If we are to receive the end of His Word, the message of salvation, we must also embrace the beginning of His Word, bowing before His infinite wisdom in giving us the Old Testament as the necessary preparation for understanding the New Testament. It is those who have discarded the beginning who are discovering that without it there is no end.

ENDNOTES

1. Cornelius Van Til: The Defence of the Faith, (Philadelphia: Presbyterian & Reformed Publishing; 1967) p.33

2. R.J.Rushdoony: The Philosophy of the Christian Curriculum, (Vallecito CA: Ross House Books; 1981) p.32

3. Ken Ham: Culture Wars: Ham vs Bacon (in Creation Magazine— Vol 25. Issue 1)

4. As argued in detail by Carl Wieland in "New eyes for blind cave fish" (www.answersingenesis.org)

5. Barna research online: The year's most intriguing findings from Barna Research Studies, 15 Aug 2002

6. D.J.Smithwick: Teachers, curriculum, control, (Nehemiah Institute, Kentucky, 1998) p.5

7. Barna Research Online—www.barna.org: "Survey shows faith impacts some behaviours not others" (22 Oct 2002)

8. G.Barna: Real Teens, (Ventura CA: Regal Books; 2001) p.136

Part 6

The Outcome of our Curriculum:

Christian Education Trains for Victory rather than Escapism

Chapter 11

Who Wins?

Our consideration of curriculum concludes with a brief exploration of eschatology, the study of the last things. What, you may ask, has that got to do with Christian education?

Eschatology, while being endlessly fascinating as evidenced in the massive success of recent novels about being left behind after Jesus' second coming, is also hugely divisive. The traditional views of eschatology are pre-millennialism, a-millennialism, and post-millennialism. The distinction between them centers on our understanding of the millennium. This, as somebody once quipped, is the thousand years of peace that Christians fight about. Another wit suggested that the only solution to the complexities of conflicting systems of interpretation would be found in pan-millennialism—the simple hope that it will all pan out in the end.

A book on Christian education is not the place to examine the intricacies of the various schools of eschatological thought. We are not seeking to persuade readers to adopt a particular eschatological viewpoint. Our goal is more practical than that. It is to suggest that the way we view the future fundamentally affects why we teach, what we teach, and how we teach. Even those who have not thought out their own convictions concerning eschatology do have certain assumptions concerning their expectations of the world of tomorrow. Those assumptions significantly affect their view of education.

History is often viewed as a battle between good and evil. This assessment is far from accurate: God has never been anything other than victorious throughout history, and the outcome has never been in doubt. However, it does provide us with a convenient framework to help us to clarify our eschatology, however inadequately thought out it might be. We may not be able to articulate the details of the system of eschatology that we have adopted, and we may not know the intricacies of the historic views of other schools of thought. But at some intuitive level, all of us would be able to say what we think (or perhaps, in a post-modern age, feel) about the answers to two fundamental questions:

* Do we win?

* How long is the fight?

These are the core issues at stake in eschatology. None would dispute that the Christian life, and the realm of Christian education in particular, is a battlefield. But the answers to these two questions radically affect how we posture ourselves on the battleground.

Firstly, do we expect to win? That is the focus of this chapter. Are we engaged in the task of Christian education with the hope of working toward a culture radically transformed into a society that demonstrates God's glory? Are we training winners? Or are we turning up on the playing field for the honor of wearing the team colors, playing no more than a spoiling role? If we anticipate the defeat of the gospel in the culture, are we more interested in providing our young people with a way of escape from overwhelming godlessness than in training them to be overcomers?

Secondly, how long is the fight? This will be our theme in the next chapter. Is the contest a marathon or a sprint; is it twelve long rounds in the ring or a cameo appearance? Is our best hope to try to ensure that our students don't get "left behind" when the Lord imminently appears? Or, are we training them to become leaders in society 50 years from now, and perhaps even more significantly, grandparents of the leaders of the 22nd Century? What, how, and why we teach should all be radically affected by the answers we give to such questions. That's why eschatology is so important.

Winners and Losers

Frank Peretti's novels have become hugely popular. That is because they reflect a mindset within the Christian community in which life in the world is seen as a battle. Of course, this coincides with the clear teaching of Scripture that we are to "fight the good fight" and that there is an enemy at work. But it is less clear that this warfare mindset accurately reflects the nature of the battle as depicted in the Bible. Perhaps it reflects a way of looking at the world that has been popularized in decades of TV programs.

The older generation was raised on Westerns; the next generation—Star Trek. It makes little difference, for the plot is essentially the same. The good guys beat the bad guys. But only just! It is politically incorrect to talk this way now, but the cowboys, in white hats, used to be the good guys. They bravely held on, constantly living with the prospect of defeat, but holding on until the cavalry finally arrived. Then the scene shifted to the final frontier: space. The battle between good and evil became intergalactic, but it was the same story line that kept the next generation on the edge of their seats until the end of the show. We boldly went back to the same plot where our fathers had gone before!

Sadly, many Christians base their theology on Star Trek and Westerns. They seem such wholesome family shows with none of the swearing and sex from which we try to shield our children. And even the violence is acceptable if directed at aliens from outer space who do not seem to bleed so profusely. In any case, violence may even be considered exemplary if in a good cause. Black and White Westerns reflect an era not only of no color on our TV screens, but a time when moral issues also seemed to be black and white. They seemed thoroughly moral in their portrayal of the triumph of good over evil. In Christian terms, Calvary is the spiritual equivalent of the cavalry. Or perhaps, in more recent novels popular among Christians, the rapture replaces the rescue by the cavalry (and, some would say, also replaces Calvary as the pivotal point of human history!).

But this is fundamentally flawed:

We dare not have a "Star Wars" theology which sees history as a cosmic battle between good and evil, with good triumphing, but only just and at the last minute, rather against the run of play. History is not a process of war against evil as God strives with man to overcome the wayward universe. History is the masterful creative handiwork of God whose throne is eternally secure. From before the beginning of time, God had a marvelous plan. Calvary is part of the plan: The Lamb was slain "*...before the foundation of the world*" (Revelation 13:8), not as a late response to an unforeseen emergency.[1]

All agree that there is a battle raging. In this chapter we consider three different expectations held by Christians about the winners and losers in this battle:

1. Some Expect to Lose!

No Christians expect to lose ultimately. But so far as life on earth is concerned, the defeat of the gospel is the expectation of many. Their "blessed hope" is the second coming that paves the way for victory in eternity, but they have little hope for victory in time and space.

A Novel Idea of Eschatology

This view has become predominant in many Christian circles, but it was once considered a novel idea. As recently as 1840, J.N. Darby proposed a *new* eschatology which suggested that any expectation of the earth being filled with the knowledge of the glory of the Lord prior to the second coming was illusory; he warned Christians to expect the growth of evil in the world. Darby admitted that this was a new idea, though it has become widespread today. In his lecture, he went on to say, "We are to expect evil until it becomes so flagrant that it will be necessary for the Lord to judge it [...] I am afraid that many a cherished feeling dear to the children of God has been shocked this evening; I mean their hope that the gospel will spread by itself over the whole earth during the actual dispensation."[2]

Darby acknowledged these ideas to be novel, and they did not go unchallenged. They were strongly resisted by Charles Spurgeon. In a sermon on Psalm 86:9, (KJV) "*All nations whom thou hast made shall*

come and worship before thee, O LORD; and shall glorify thy name,"
Spurgeon warned against the paralyzing consequences of such views
being introduced as he expounded the Scripture's expectation of a
glorious kingdom on earth. "David was not a believer," said Spurgeon,
"in the *modern* theory that the world will grow worse and worse, and that
the dispensation will wind up with general darkness and idolatry. Earth's
sun is to go down amidst tenfold night if some of our prophetic brethren
[men like Darby in Spurgeon's day] are to be believed. Not so do we
expect! But we look for a day when the dwellers in all lands shall learn
righteousness, shall trust in the saviour, shall worship thee alone, O God,
'and shall glorify thy name.'"[3]

These views of Darby and Spurgeon represent a debate on eschatology that began as recently as the nineteenth century. Unfortunately,
Darby's views have been widely embraced, perhaps because they were
spread in the first, and still most popular, study Bible, by C.I. Scofield,
a study Bible that has molded the doctrine of generations of Christians.
So now pessimism is rampant. William Hendrickson asserted that the
gospel age "will finally result in the complete destruction of the church
as a mighty and influential organization for the spread of the gospel."
Ironically, this statement appears in his commentary entitled "More
than Conquerors!"

But what has this to do with education? Such a view, consistently
applied, militates against all forms of Christian education.

An Eschatology of Shipwreck

It is this view that has led countless believers to opt out of pursuing
further education, and this view has led to the mass exodus of
Christians from involvement in many aspects of public life. It is one
reason why most of the key positions in education, politics, law, and
other areas of professional life have been vacated by Christians and
taken over by humanists. If there is no hope for making any lasting
changes in the state of the world, the Christian's obvious response is to
withdraw and retreat.

In the 1960's, Hal Lindsay's massive best seller *Late Great Planet
Earth* persuaded a whole generation that current events of the day in the
Middle East proved that the second coming was imminent (no later than
1987 according to his calculations at the time, though he didn't go quite

so far as to state that explicitly—which, fortunately for him, has meant that he can continue to publish later editions). With the revival emerging at that time among the "Jesus people," countless Christian young people dropped out of school and many decided that it would be irresponsible to have children. These decisions arose out of their eschatology.

Why? Because they were convinced that the world was going to become so bad that it would be unbearable for children if Jesus' return was delayed. But delay was not expected, and thus, with so little time left, it was considered a waste of precious time to devote years to study for a profession that they would never enter. The urgent need was not for lawyers and teachers who would fill positions of influence forty years later; after all, the problems of the world would at that time be left for those who are "left behind" to worry about! The urgent need was for evangelism.

None can criticize a passionate commitment to evangelism. But this was evangelism driven by what has been described as an "eschatology of shipwreck." Instead of trying to build anything of lasting value in society, the impetus was to jump from the sinking ship of humanism and to take to the lifeboats. The only hope is the hope of the life vest: personal salvation for the individuals who can be persuaded to jump, who will make it to the far shore while the world is left to sink. Why waste valuable time trying to shore up to a dying culture when there are souls to save?

We are paying the price for that philosophy. The defeatist vision that led Christians to withdraw from the world has meant that as we have left the battlefield, the humanists have been winning by default. They now hold most of the key positions.

Some Christians are beginning to wake up, realizing that the end did not come quite as suddenly as we had expected in the 60's, though the *Left Behind* books are now doing for the present generation what Lindsay's books did for an earlier generation. But since the Rapture did not happen as was expected, our freedoms as Christians are being eroded and our children are being bombarded with overwhelming worldliness. Now, even those who expect defeat are beginning to think about Christian education as a place of temporary safety while awaiting the true safety of our eternal rescue. This is not the vision for Christian education that we are proposing. Those whose eschatology is essentially pessimistic have a view of Christian education that might be somewhat unfairly caricatured as "Lifeboat Education."

Lifeboat education is a view of Christian education that sees home-schooling or the Christian school as a means of escape, a way out for parents who are concerned about the effects of a sinking ship on their children. In contrast, the vision of Christian education we are outlining is not geared toward enabling children to escape from a dying world, but toward equipping them to serve a dying world. They are to serve a dying world, not just dying individuals. As Dennis Peacocke has pointed out, it is strange that the church should spend so much energy thinking about escaping from the world when God spent eternity planning how to get into the world! And still God's plan is for the earth to be filled with the knowledge of the glory of the Lord.

If we believed in the inevitable self-destruction of this sinful world, and if we knew with certainty that the second coming would occur within a generation, there would be far more pressing needs on which to spend resources than operating a Christian school.

2. Some Expect to win—but Only Spiritually!

Not all Christians are pessimistic in their expectations of the future. But many who regard themselves as optimistic still see that optimism in apparently "spiritual" terms; this may effectively still leave the "real world" in the hands of the kingdom of darkness.

Revivals and Missions

Particularly in charismatic circles, there has been a renewed interest in revival in recent decades. Sometimes that hope has been couched in terms of expecting a significant end-times harvest, an idea that was popularized a generation or two ago in the talk about "latter rain." In recent years, much attention in such circles has focused particularly on the role of young people in that expectation, with renewed talk of the "terminal generation" and the excitement that a radical youth culture will usher in the return of the Lord.

In more conservative circles, the same idea revolves around missions rather than revival. Toward the end of the twentieth century, many began to strategize to take the gospel to all the unreached people-groups by the year 2000. The mystique of the new millennium has now passed, but the urgency of taking the gospel into all the world continues. The strategies to plan cooperative global missions to realize that goal within this generation remain as determined as ever. There is a significant eschatological dimension in this thrust: most agree that the Lord will not return until the gospel has been taken to all the tribes and languages on earth. Thus, the urgency to take the gospel into untouched territory is part of hastening the second coming.

If this is a primary focus for the church, there are significant implications for Christian education. Like our brethren who expect the failure of the gospel to transform the culture as a whole, the need within this missions focus is also on evangelism. All available resources must be made available to take the gospel to as many as possible in the shortest time possible. Why would we be training young people for careers as accountants or plumbers if the need is for evangelists? Why would we seek to prepare them for the long haul if the goal is to get the job done as quickly as possible? The answers to these questions ultimately come down to our definition of the gospel and our assumptions about eschatology.

The gospel is most commonly seen in terms of personal salvation. In that case, the goal is to reach as many people as possible, in as many parts of the world as possible, with the good news about Jesus' offer of forgiveness of sins through His death, thereby adding them to the church and assuring them of a place in heaven. According to this view, the Church's Great Commission will be complete when as many as possible have prayed the sinner's prayer. Little emphasis may be placed on the discipleship of those new converts beyond enrolling them quickly in the army of those busy making new converts, and little emphasis is placed on the implications for a whole society as larger numbers of its members become Christians and seek to live the whole of their lives under Jesus' Lordship.

Converting Individuals or Changing Nations?

If the gospel is the gospel of the Kingdom, as the New Testament teaches, rather than simply a gospel of personal salvation, the Great Commission is both more complex and more long-term than might otherwise be assumed. It would seem that Jesus seeks the salvation of the world, the whole created order, not just a lot of individuals, the whole created order continues to groan awaiting the freedom that will come when the sons of God come into their own. The climax of history is not the final individual sinner placing his trust in Jesus, but the whole earth being filled with the knowledge of God's glory. If Jesus is not simply returning to a large number of believers, but to a world that is full of believers who have brought their lives under his Lordship and in turn have transformed the wilderness into a place of glorious fruit as they have learned to live life on earth the way God planned for them to do, then the task is vast. Taking the bare necessities of the "Four Spiritual Laws" to a sufficient number of representative individuals so that we can say that the gospel has gone to all the world may be achievable in a few decades, but the transformation of the nations to the point that it can be said that "All nations whom thou hast made shall come and worship before thee, O Lord; and shall glorify thy name" (as Spurgeon proclaimed from Psalm 86) may take many centuries!

It all comes down to the nature of the gospel. Is the gospel primarily "spiritual" in the sense that it is a matter of saving souls, adding to the Church, and assuring people of a place in heaven? Or does the gospel affect all of life and the whole created order? In Part 2 we proposed that the notion of a spiritual/secular dichotomy is a serious misconception. The goal of Christian education is to focus on the kingdom of God rather than a narrower pietistic view of personal salvation.

To take this a step further, the preoccupation with saving souls, when that precludes the further dimensions of discipleship, may even hinder the progress of the gospel of the Kingdom. The Great Commission requires us to make disciples, not converts. As we saw in Chapter 3, the Great Commission, along with the earlier but intrinsically related Dominion Mandate, form the *raison d'être* for Christian education. There may be some debate as to whether, when Jesus told us to *make disciples of all the nations*," He had in mind the active discipleship of whole nations in God's ways, as opposed to discipling representative individuals from all the nations. But there should be no doubt that when significant numbers of individuals are discipled in "*all* that He commands," as opposed to being discipled only in the things that he Hays about soul-winning, there will be profound changes in whole nations. It is to that end that Christian education should raise its sights.

As the focus in the Christian world moves toward the urgency of the missionary mandate and the prospect of the current generation of young people being the terminal generation of evangelists, the pressure on Christian schools becomes to produce graduates whose goal is to attend Bible College, or some less formal or more short-term training program. Home-schooling parents desire that their children will be equipped to sign up for one of the ever-growing number of youth-oriented missions organizations, enrolling in this army of end-time Christian workers. Surely we would not want to discourage the most spiritual and fervent of our students pursuing such a laudable goal.

Undoubtedly the Church and the massive task of world missions need some of our brightest and best students. To use the terminology we developed earlier, the task of building the "temple" is very important, and some of our students will be called to a life of service in these areas. But we are also called to build a "city" (a holistic vision for society, not just the "spiritual" dimension of church), and it is in the life of the city where the significant cultural transformation is to be worked out.

The apparently spiritual careers of being a pastor or a missionary are no more prestigious than other careers. Our task in Christian education is to enthuse all of our students to see that they can make a difference in the world wherever God calls them. The most spiritual career choice is the one which God directs. That may be as a city-dweller, or as a temple-dweller. The city-dweller has the privilege of taking the gospel of the Kingdom into realms such as politics and law, business and manufacturing.

For those who are called to the city, a few years in Bible College or in a missions program may actually leave them already behind their non-Christian peers if they are to become qualified to fill positions of influence. We should not hinder their progress into their callings. We will effectively motivate students who are called to serve the Lord in careers in professions or in trades when we instill in them an eschatological conviction that God's people are called to the world. Going into all the world does not only mean going to all the geographical regions of the world; it also entails going into all the spheres of influence in the world. This is a high calling if we have an eschatological hope of cultural transformation.

3. Some Expect to Win!

Implicit in the vision of Christian education presented in this book is the expectation that we win! We are not pouring our energy into the lives of young people expecting them to face inevitable defeat. We are anticipating that the fruit of our sowing in their young lives will be reaped in a harvest that includes both multitudes of saved souls *and* effectively transformed cultures. As Iain Murray points out in his book "The Puritan Hope,"[4] it was the expectation of the earth being filled with the knowledge of the glory of the Lord that gave birth to the missionary movement that exploded into life at the end of the eighteenth century. That same hope compels us to invest heavily in Christian education.

What a Hope!

The "hope" of the Puritans, to which Murray refers in the title of his book, is the hope of the triumph of the gospel. This has a broader scope than the salvation of souls. The hope that took William Carey to India was the firm conviction that the entire continent would one day bow the knee to the Lord Jesus. This was the same hope that stirred the Pilgrim fathers somewhat earlier. It was the hope, as we noted earlier, that John Winthrop articulated on board the *Arabella* just prior to landing in the New World, when he anticipated the settlers being involved in the glorious prospect of becoming a "city set on a hill."

The Puritan vision of the Christian life was driven by a desire to see pure practical Christianity throughout all of life, public or private, whether in the home, the church, at work, or in civil affairs. Their desire was not only to produce good pastors and missionaries, but successful Christian businessmen and productive citizens and godly civil servants who had the integrity to govern justly. For them, as Overman points out, "social and cultural involvement was […] the natural outgrowth of a worldview which saw all of life as sacred, and everything under the dominion of God."[5]

How different is the Puritan vision of building a city set on the hill from modern evangelicalism's desire to evacuate the city! I refer to "evacuate" in the sense of ceasing to expect to play a role in a city's formation, and replacing that with a raiding party mentality which ventures into the city just to snatch others out of it, saving them for the world to come. Christian teachers must articulate and model the truth that all of life is to be lived to the glory of God. Christian education must persuade our young people that to succeed in a profession or a trade is as valid as so-called "full-time ministry."

Is Withdrawal from Secular Education Escapism?

In Christian schools and the home-schooling movement we pull our children out of the world's system in order to educate them in a secure Christian environment. This can easily become the breeding ground for an escapist mindset. There may be valid grounds for withdrawing our children in this way. But that conviction must not become the basis for assuming that all of life is to be lived in isolation from the world.

The simple analogy that illustrates that withdrawal is necessary, but only as a temporary measure, is that of the greenhouse. Our children, like plants, are sheltered from the rigors of the world's climate in order to grow a strong enough root system to be able to survive when subsequently planted out in the world. But our children must know that the greenhouse is not the environment for which they were created. They must understand that they are being prepared for life in the world—a life in which they will have to survive all kinds of storms and pressures, but a life in which they are called to be fruitful.

A significant biblical model in this regard was Abraham. He raised his household in a wilderness setting. This proved to be a wise move in comparison to his nephew Lot's decision to raise his children in the city. Christian parents have an obligation to protect their children from the influences of Sodom; they fail to do so at their own peril. But the life in the wilderness is not an end in itself. Abraham's mandate was always that the families *of the world* would be blessed through his offspring (Genesis 12:3). Those trained in the security of that protected environment were the ones who were ready, when the time came, to take on the world system that was proving to be so destructive in Abraham's day.

It was the graduates of this secluded "household of faith" training program in the wilderness who were equipped to go and rescue Lot and his imprisoned family, as the story unfolds in Genesis 14. As parents contemplate the prospect of Christian education, it should be with a view to training warriors who will be victorious in the city, not weak specimens that can only survive in the greenhouse. All that is taught must be geared toward preparing our young people for the real world, though ironically that is often best accomplished in the artificial environment of the greenhouse, which remains a secure place until the roots of character development and core beliefs have become so established that they will be able to weather any storm. But the vision of battles to fight and a world to win must always be held before our students lest they settle down complacently to the comforts of life in the Temple without a hunger to be involved in building a city.

ENDNOTES

1. Brian Watts: The Treasure in the Field (Upper Hutt NZ: Spirit of Truth; 1995) p.11f

2. Quoted by Iain Murray: The Puritan Hope (London: Banner of Truth; 1975) p.156

3. CH Spurgeon: The Treasury of David (London: Passmore & Alabaster; 1875), Vol IV p.102

4. Iain Murray: The Puritan Hope—A study in revival and the interpretation of prophecy (London: Banner of Truth; 1971)

5. Christian Overman,: Assumptions that Affect our Lives (Chatsworth CA: Micah 6:8; 1996) p.230

Chapter 12

How long?

Not only does eschatology determine our answer to the question, "Who wins?" as we discussed in the previous chapter. It also has a bearing on the length of the battle.

Christian education is all about training. Training is only effective when it has a particular goal in mind, and the training program suitable for running a marathon is very different than the training program that will enable somebody to be a successful sprinter. So teachers who are involved in the training business must be able to answer the question of whether we are training for short term or long term outcomes. Again, different Christians with different eschatologies will come up with different answers. Here are three of them.

1. We Lose—Soon!

Some of our more pessimistic friends think mostly within a short-term mindset. The world is getting so bad that, in the minds of many, the end must be both inevitable and imminent. I recall, as a child, being exposed week after week to preaching that expounded the imminent return of the Lord because of the Arab-Israeli conflicts that were then filling the news.

I remember praying with great intensity on one occasion in the early summer that the Lord would delay his return until September so that we could enjoy the family holiday that was planned for August!

What context does this establish for career planning? What possible relevance could any of my studies have for a life about to be cut short by an imminent second coming? Why would I think about embarking on further education? I did go to university, but not with any clear career plan in mind; it was just the most obvious next thing to do to fill in the time. As a result I sailed through school and university without ever thinking that what I was learning had any relevance to real life, to my plans for the future, or to my Christian faith, which was very real and sincere, but was limited entirely to church life and occasional forays into the world for evangelism. Nobody who expects the Lord's return to cut off hope of a summer vacation will pour the necessary time and resources into pioneering a Christian school.

2. We Win—Soon!

But even amongst those of us who anticipate a victorious conclusion to the progress of the gospel in human history, there are significant differences of opinion as to how long this is all going to take. As we have pointed out, there is a growing view, encouraged by certain prophetic emphases within the charismatic movement, that we are on the verge of a great revival, and history will be wound up with a glorious, soon to be realized, victory. There are several cautions that need to be maintained in light of this view:

* Are we Looking for Discontinuity or Continuity?

The danger of such a view is that it is always looking for the big break-through. That big break-through comes suddenly from outside rather than gradually from within. In terms of biblical interpretation, it would seem that Jesus' teaching on the Kingdom stresses the importance of gradualism, of slow but steady growth, of faithfully sowing and watering and watching the process ripen toward harvest. But we live in an era that sees hope in the radical, the revolutionary, the sudden disruption of all that has been. Whether that radical discontinuity is the sudden return of the Lord or the sudden outpouring of the Holy Spirit, there is something in the modern psyche that yearns for an instant solution to the world's problems, just as our love of microwave dinners reflects our yearning for instant solutions to another kind of hunger!

But we need to train our young people, in a counter-cultural manner, in the importance of faithfulness in the long haul, of persevering when there are no apparent results, in the importance of a consistent work ethic that expects nothing that we are not prepared to work for. How many of our young people expect, when they are married, to instantly have all the modern conveniences that their parents worked for years to be able to afford? How many expect to have high-paying jobs and a comfortable standard of living as soon as they leave school or college? How many expect success and recognition as a right rather than a privilege that is earned over a long time? How many understand the biblical teaching of sowing and reaping rather than expecting the consequences of their mistakes and foolishness to be instantly wiped out as if by a magic wand? How many will still be serving God faithfully in 50 years time, even if there is no excitement and novelty to keep them going?

As people look for the dramatic intervention more and more, rather than to the fruitfulness of faithful perseverance, they are vulnerable in two possible directions. On the one hand, disillusionment sets in as the expectations of the momentous event fade after seeing a succession of promising "new waves" come and go. Or, alternatively, in the hunger for the elusive once-for-all breakthrough, people become increasingly vulnerable to the deceptions of bizarre counterfeits that seem to offer instant solutions. Young people need to be trained to be patient and persevering, with a commitment to the long haul. This is the only antidote against both disillusion and deception.

* Are Young People the Answer to the World's Problems?

Christian young people today are being bombarded by the message that they are special. That is sometimes communicated in prophetic terms as they are referred to as the generation that will usher in the return of the Lord. Frequently it is communicated in the educational attempts to protect their supposedly fragile self-esteem with encouraging words that prevent them from having to face failure or even mediocrity. And it is seen in a church culture that is increasingly geared to their preferences and desires rather than those of the older generation; the older folks seem content to put up with novelty and music styles as long as they are encouraged to see young people in their services.

But is this healthy? And is it biblical? Gone are the days when the young would rise in respect as an older person entered the room. While younger people may be more adept with the latest technological developments, are they really smarter and wiser than their parents? Ronald Reagan was once interrupted by a young man while he was speaking at a college about the state of the world. The student taunted the former president by saying that his generation could not possibly understand: they had, after all, grown up without computers, television, microwaves, space travel. Reagan's retort silenced him: "We invented those things!"

And while the zeal of today's youth is important as it is directed towards the advancement of Christ's kingdom, does that zeal really compare well with the passion of earlier generations, whose love for the Lord may not have been so demonstrative in terms of worship styles, but was far more willing to pay a price either in physical suffering or in the demands of holiness? We may be doing young people a disservice when we tell them they are so special, so smart, so capable—either educationally or spiritually.

This counter-cultural message needs to be communicated to our young people. If it is not, many will be tempted to fall away if their generation proves not to be the great solution, especially if, at that time, there is a new generation that has taken on the mantle of being the special ones. In the inevitable law of sowing and reaping, a generation that is now showing its disdain for its parents' generation will reap the disdain of its own children in time. Their best hope is not in thinking of themselves as unique, but in taking their place in the continuum of history, serving the Lord in their generation as they honor those who have gone before and prepare the way for those who will follow. A child-centered education is eschatologically unsound. It fails to reflect the big picture of God's long term, multi-generational purposes.

3. We Win—but Maybe not Yet!

Disillusionment is a significant factor in people falling away from their love for the Lord. Hope, as we saw in the Puritans, is a wonderful motivator. But the Bible is also clear: "*Hope deferred makes the heart sick*" (Proverbs 13:12). There are many whose hopes were aroused in the early days of the charismatic movement, and in the anticipation of the

60's and 70's for an imminent return of the Lord, who have now given up waiting for the hope that proved to be always just around the corner.

This is not a new phenomenon. Paul wrote to first generation Christians in Thessalonica who were discouraged that some of their number had started to die. They had expected Jesus to come back long before they got old. But the fact that believers through the centuries have faced the disappointments of life not working out as their theology led them to hope does not excuse us from the responsibility of helping our young people prepare for a life of perseverance. A long-term perspective is becoming increasingly rare.

Embarking on Long-term Projects

How different this was in earlier centuries. The mindset was certainly not short term when a European community embarked on building a cathedral, committed to seeing the knowledge of the glory of the Lord filling the earth. They knew that they were starting a project that could take centuries to complete. Nonetheless, they considered it worthwhile to embark upon despite the fact that the first builders would never live to see the completed project.

Perhaps they understood that God is a God of three generations (the God of Abraham, Isaac, and Jacob); they saw their personal destiny within the broader context of a past heritage and a future inheritance. The achievements of Abraham's life seemed little more than a burial plot, certainly not the promised city, other than the offspring who would later bring the promised blessings to fruition. And with that perspective in mind, our forefathers embarked on great building programs regardless of the prospects for their own enjoyment of the fruit of their labors.

One of the first things the great historic cathedral builders would do was to plant an orchard of acorns. They knew that in the final stages of construction, oak trees would be needed to provide timber for pews. They knew that they would never live to see those trees come to maturity, but they were planning for the long haul. Similarly, the building process was not a race to get as many stones up as fast as possible. They knew that they would never see the building finished, so the more important task was for the stonemasons to train their sons to be able to continue building after them, and to train them to be able to train their sons too, for it would often take those three generations to complete the task. How different than the culture of our day, though entirely consistent with Paul's multi-generational approach to church-building (2 Timothy 2:1,2)!

In Christian education, regardless of the theory of our eschatology, we are taking a multi-generational view. We do not invest our time in our personal agenda, but devote ourselves to those whom we train. They will be trained to do things that we will never be able to do, in times and places where we will never go. Parents choose to draw back from what they might otherwise be doing in order to equip their children to be able to do more later. We need to impart not only the skills that we can teach our young people, but the mindset that enables them to see that all is not lost if they do not accomplish all their goals in their life-time, so long as they are also part of the process of training future generations. We need to impart the perspective that there is more to success in life than what an individual personally accomplishes. As Paul puts it, there is a whole chain of sowing and planting and watering which requires a lot of people who will never personally see the fruit of their labors. There is much more to life than what one person gets out of it or what one person achieves.

I wonder whether any of our students would ever consider spending their life on a project like building a cathedral, which they knew at the outset they would never see finished? The fact is that there are many such outstanding projects that will take at least as long.

When idealistic humanists set out to transform the education system into a tool for their social agenda, they knew that they were embarking on a multi-generational task. They dreamed of the day in which we live, a day when the educational system had become the breeding ground for secular thought. But they themselves never saw it.

It would be naïve to think that a thoroughly Christian system of education can be accomplished any quicker. Replacing the current crumbling educational system may take longer than building a cathedral. And it is probably an even larger project to embark on restoring, for example, a health-care system on biblical foundations. But does that mean that our young people should desert the sinking ship of current institutions in the city of man, giving themselves to projects with more visible short-term outcomes? Our civilization is built on the foundations of those who were willing to work toward goals that they themselves would never see fulfilled. The cause was bigger than their own sense of accomplishment.

Success—Here or There?

We have spoken of an optimistic outcome of human history. There can be no doubt biblically that one day the earth will be filled with the knowledge of the glory of the Lord. But does that mean that it is inevitable that life will get endlessly brighter and more glorious for our children? Not necessarily—in fact, not likely! The tide in our Western culture at this point is clearly moving away from its Christian roots; secularism and humanism are coming in like a flood. It would be wonderful if a mighty revival stemmed that tide, as has been the case in numerous instances throughout history. But there are other instances where the church in a locality at a particular time has been over-run by the kingdom of darkness. We cannot pretend that the Church in the West deserves anything less in our day.

We live in days of phenomenal success in the advance of the gospel. We may not always see it that way, living in the increasingly anti-Christian West. But robust, dynamic Christianity is spreading like wildfire across the globe; or at least, across Latin America, Africa, and much of Asia. On a global scale, Christianity is anything but in retreat from the attacks of secular humanism. As Philip Jenkins points out in his significant book *The Next Christendom: The Coming of Global Christianity*[1], we are reaching the point where Europe and North America cease to be the focal point of the faith.

This indisputable fact has implications. Firstly, if we are training our young people to be cultural transformers, we need to realize that the more successful models of such transformation may well take place outside our culture. Our young people, in being trained to be part of seeing God's glory fill the earth, need to have a global perspective and a missions focus.

But secondly, this does not mean that we should all be looking across the ocean. Rather, while retaining an overall optimism for the advance of the gospel, many must face the fact that their lives may be spent in a context of decline, which, in effect, is an expression of the judgment of God. Like the Jews born in captivity in Babylon, the judgment may not be on their personal sin, but on the culture of which they are a part. But even living in a modern equivalent of Babylon does not permit a mindset of escapism. God's people were still encouraged to be "city-builders," settling down and seeking the welfare of the city in which they found themselves, godless as it was. So Jeremiah encouraged them with the perspective of the long haul (see Jeremiah 29: 5-7,28; 40:9). The shining example of success in the gospel may be elsewhere at this point in time; but we are called to be faithful where God has placed us.

Suffering—Here or There?

Believing in victory in the long run does not mean ignoring the possibility of defeat in the short run, at least, defeat in a particular part of the world at a particular time. It may be that the young people currently in our schools face a future that is darker than anything we have had to face. Are we preparing them for the possibility of suffering? Or are we leading them to believe that all is getting better and better—evolution at work in our thinking—and that they are God's favored spoiled ones who, unlike His precious saints in China and elsewhere, will never be called upon to feel pain?

We think of success "here" and hardship "there"—in some distant place. In much current eschatological thinking, this Western-centered assumption drives the belief in the inevitability of an imminent Rapture. It is said to be unthinkable that God would allow his loved ones to suffer the coming tribulation, so it is inevitable that the Rapture must occur to take us out before it gets too bad. Try telling that to those whom He chose not to Rapture out of their tribulations in Soviet or Chinese torture chambers. No, the reality may be that in the increasing globalization of Christianity we face the prospect of the unparalleled success of the gospel in the world at large, while simultaneously experiencing the greatest resistance to the gospel here in the West. Success may be moving from here to there, and suffering from there to here! How do we prepare our students for an increasingly hostile world and a lifetime of battles?

Ironically, the best preparation for conflict and suffering is an eschatology of victory. Confidence in Christ's victory in the long haul best serves this end. To know that we win makes all the difference in engaging in the battle. Whatever we might be called upon to suffer is worthwhile if we can be sure that the victory is promised. We will step onto the battlefield and play a heroic role when we know that what is important is not our personal comfort, but the ultimate glory of God in the earth. It may be that the standard by which the success of today's Christian education movement will be measured is the yardstick of whether we produced heroes who are up for the fight and committed to the cause of the glory of the Lord even when all around appeared dark.

We have seen that curriculum is all about the course. It outlines the race that has to be run. Preparing students for the race-track of life requires training that enables them to press through pain. The successful curriculum is the one which enables students to press through to the end of the race, and, when the course is over, to hear the commendation of the Lord, *"Well done, good and faithful servants!"*

ENDNOTES

1. Philip Jenkins: The Next Christendom: The coming of global Christianity (Oxford University Press; 2002)

Books to help you grow strong in Jesus

MY LEGACY
By Rowan McRae

My Legacy is an interactive journal that asks simple but provocative questions and will inspire you to remember important events, circumstances, and feelings in your own life. It also provides an incentive to evaluate your time used thus far and how to make better use of the time you have left. Presented as a unique gift to older loved ones, this journal will encourage them to pass along their heritage to you and future generations. What a great gift in return as you learn from their experiences and discover the importance and value of the treasured moments of their life. ISBN:88-89127-06-6

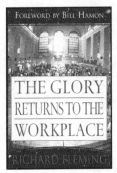

THE GLORY RETURNS TO THE WORKPLACE
By Richard Fleming

More than 90% of all Christians know that their purpose and their vision from God lies outside the pulpit of the local church. Unfortunately, few know how to release the vision and walk in it successfully. *The Glory Returns to The Workplace* unveils God's strategies in a clear and practical way as stepping-stones to help you walk into the fullness of your call and destiny. You will be challenged to allow God's presence to be manifested in your life—right in your job—as you allow the gifts and power of God's Spirit to flow through your life and into the lives of others. ISBN:88-89127-04-X

OVERCOMING TEMPTATION
By Manickam Chandrakumar

God has given us the power and the desire to resist the work of the enemy. Sin does not have to be a normal way of life. You can learn how to resist the temptation that leads to sin. The author has helped people in over sixty countries with the principles in this book. You can turn your defeat into victory, no matter how strong the temptation to sin might be in your life. This book will give you the keys to begin a life of true victory! ISBN:88-89127-03-1

Order Now from Destiny Image Europe
Telephone: +39 085 4716623- Fax +39 085 4716622
E-mail: ordini@eurodestinyimage.com

Internet: www.eurodestinyimage.com

WHERE ARE THE SONS IN THE HOUSE?

By Jerome Nel

Within the church, the concept of mentoring has existed throughout the ages. Spiritual fathers mentor their sons-both men and women-who then become fathers to the next generation. *Where are the Sons in the House?* examines the vital relationship of mentors (spiritual fathers) and mentees (spiritual sons and daughters) in the house of God. This book will allow you to clearly see your role in the local church and will inspire and challenge you to meet your full potential as a member of the body of Christ. This book will open your eyes to the truth of how satan so often manipulates the body of Christ and hinders her growth. If you are serious about becoming who God intends you to be, you must read this book! ISBN:88-89127-01-5

THE HOLE IN THE HEDGE

By Mario Marchiò

"*The Hole in the Hedge*" will help the reader understand the vital truth found in Scripture which states, "He who breaks a hedge, a snake will bite him!" The author brings clarity and solace where there was confusion and doubt while bringing you one step closer to the reality of the Gospel of Jesus Christ, which is, "God is good and He loves me." ISBN:88-89127-00-7

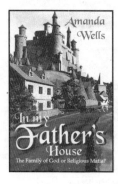

IN MY FATHER'S HOUSE

By Amanda Wells

Too many men of God today are deceived into a building a pedestal, whereby, they have to keep other men from either dethroning them or climbing on board with them. This is not about pride and arrogance. Let it never become about numbers, who has more, but let this apostolic move be about lives and the shaping of men and women into their God-given call and destinies, who leave an inheritance and legacy for our sons and daughters to walk in. ISBN: 88-900588-6-2

TRANSFORMATION AND DOMINION

By Lee LaCoss

Jesus says, "...upon this rock, I will build My church..." In this book we discover many ways that Jesus accomplishes this purpose in and through His people. We are confronted with real questions and issues, and are given practical, biblical answers and direction.

The Lord's "new creation humanity" is called to know Him, and to mature by expressing His nature and abilities as true overcomes in this life.

ISBN: 88-900588-7-0

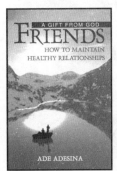

FRIENDS, A GIFT FROM GOD
How to Maintain Healthy Relationships

By Ade Adesina

Relationships are fundamental in the race of life; they can easily be the making or conversely the breaking of any man. All seem to agree that, "no man is an island", however the solution is also often the problem, for the mismanagement of these relationships can negatively impact one's destiny. Many are living frustrated lives because of mismanaged relationships. Pastor Adesina in this insightful study, expatiates on the nature, purpose and modes of operation of the different types of relationships, and with practical steps, he places in one's hands the tools necessary to enjoy a healthy relationship with all. It is possible...discover now. ISBN: 88-900588-8-9

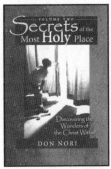

SECRETS OF THE MOST HOLY PLACE: VOL. 2

By Don Nori

Heaven is my destination, but it is not my destiny. Many will reach their destination, but few will achieve their destiny. Prophetic parable matures into prophetic reality as His presence draws us into the realm of 'all God.' Here, what we believe becomes what we experience and what we know becomes flesh in mere mortal man. This book is not for the casual reader. It is for those who hunger, not for education, but for reality; not for religion, but for Him. The world awaits the love of a people who know they are forgiven. ISBN: 0768421756

Order Now from Destiny Image Europe
Telephone: +39 085 4716623- Fax +39 085 4716622
E-mail: ordini@eurodestinyimage.com

Internet: www.eurodestinyimage.com